THE SUPREME COURT
AND POLITICAL QUESTIONS

THE SUPREME COURT
AND POLITICAL QUESTIONS

By

CHARLES GORDON POST, JR.

25293

DA CAPO PRESS • NEW YORK • 1969

A Da Capo Press Reprint Edition

This Da Capo Press edition of
The Supreme Court and Political Questions
is an unabridged republication of the first
edition published in Baltimore in 1936 as
Series LIV, Number 4, of the *Johns Hopkins
University Studies in Historical and
Political Science.*

Library of Congress Catalog Card Number 74-87386

Published by Da Capo Press
A Division of Plenum Publishing Corporation
227 West 17th Street
New York, N. Y. 10011

Printed in the United States of America

THE SUPREME COURT AND POLITICAL
QUESTIONS

THE SUPREME COURT AND POLITICAL QUESTIONS

By

CHARLES GORDON POST, JR., PH. D.

Assistant Professor, Political Science
Vassar College

BALTIMORE

THE JOHNS HOPKINS PRESS

1936

PRINTED IN THE UNITED STATES OF AMERICA
BY J. H. FURST COMPANY, BALTIMORE, MARYLAND

To

EMILY DOHME POST

NOTE

It is a pleasure for the writer to acknowledge his indebtedness to several individuals, associated in the Department of Political Science at the Johns Hopkins University, who have rendered him no little assistance in the preparation of this work. Dr. Westel W. Willoughby read the manuscript and made a number of valuable suggestions. Dr. James Hart, now Professor of Political Science at the University of Virginia, not only suggested the subject of this study, but by patient criticism led the writer to rise upon the ashes of his old ways of thinking. Mr. Leon Sachs rendered a service of friendship and scholarship in reading the manuscript and giving the writer the benefit of a splendid knowledge of constitutional law. Dr. Johannes Mattern offered many suggestions and criticisms, particularly as regards style and clarity, with a most improving effect. Mrs. Victoria Golz, Secretary in the Department, read the manuscript and endured the tedious labor of checking footnotes and quotations.

It would be impossible to leave this study without an expression of gratitude to the President of Vassar College, Dr. Henry Noble MacCracken, whose kindly assistance made possible the publication of this volume.

C. G. P., Jr.

Vassar College,
August, 1936.

CONTENTS

THE SUPREME COURT AND POLITICAL QUESTIONS

CHAPTER I

INTRODUCTION

It is a well-established rule of American constitutional law that when a court is faced with the problem, let us say, of the authority of foreign ambassadors and ministers, it will disclaim all authority over the question and accept the decision of the political departments—the executive and legislative—of the government. Such a question has been called a political question by the courts. The questions of the existence of a state of war, the extent of the jurisdiction of a foreign power, the jurisdiction of the United States over an island in the high seas, the question of the validity of treaties in so far as public rights are concerned, the right of Indians to recognition as a tribe, are among the many problems considered by the courts to be included within the category of political questions, and, therefore, beyond their jurisdiction. The term "political question," itself, would seem to be what may be called an "open sesame" word. When Ali Baba approached the great iron portal which was his particular problem, all he had to say was "open sesame"; the problem was solved, and the consequences aspired to, attained. In the same manner, when a court labels a particular problem a "political question" (the magic word), though no great door swings open to reveal unlimited treasure, the court is instantly relieved of all control over the problem; the question, so far as it concerns the particular case, is removed from the jurisdiction of the court, and, ordinarily, no matter how the political departments decide the question, the court will abide by that decision.

Several reasons have been expressed or implied as constituting the *raison d'être* of political questions, none of which satisfactorily withstand analysis. Oliver P. Field, in a short

11

article, "The Doctrine of Political Questions in the Federal Courts," [1] emphatically asserts that "whatever may be the difficulties in definitively describing the differences between the judicial and the legislative department, it seems settled and clear that the court must have some rule to follow before it can operate. Where no rules exist, the court is powerless to act. From this it follows that the courts cannot enter into questions of statecraft or policy." [2] There is perhaps a degree of truth in this statement, but as an explanation of the motivating force underlying the utilization of the doctrine of political questions, it is too simple; at least, it is unsatisfactory in so far as it avoids a more realistic explanation and presumes an antiquated philosophy of law.

Mr. Justice Woodbury, in his dissenting opinion in the case of *Luther* v. *Borden*,[3] expressed the idea that political questions are not within the jurisdiction of the courts, because their determination rests with the electorate. "The adjustment of these questions," he said, "belongs to the people and their political representatives, either in the State or General Government." [4] Of course, in the adjustment of almost any governmental question, "the people and their political representatives" could stand, in theory at least, as the final court of arbitration; but the vague identity of "the people," and the shadowy relationship existing between them and their political representatives, prompts one to do no more than nod pleasantly to the "people" and pass on. As the reason underlying the application of the doctrine of political questions this *might* have been satisfactory in the particular case, but we shall see later on that even here it is not to be sustained.

Perhaps the most usual explanation for the establishment of the category of political questions is to be found in the doctrine of the separation of powers. According to this basic principle of our constitutional jurisprudence, the exercise of legislative, executive and judicial powers, must not be concentrated in one body, but in distinct and independent organs of government. The purpose of this principle is to

---

[1] *Minnesota Law Review*, VIII, 485.
[2] *Ibid.*, p. 511.   [3] 7 How. 1 (1849).   [4] *Ibid.*, 51.

protect the governed against the arbitrary or oppressive action of those individuals who enjoy the privilege of exercising political authority. As Madison said, "the accumulation of all powers Legislative, Executive, and Judiciary, in the same hands, whether of one, a few, or many, and whether hereditary, self-appointed, or elective, may justly be pronounced the very definition of tyranny." [5] The Constitution of the United States, however, contains no clause specifically distributing executive, legislative and judicial powers, but what amounts in effect to the same thing is found in the following provisions of that document: "all legislative powers herein granted shall be vested in a Congress of the United States "; [6] " the executive power shall be vested in a President "; [7] and "the judicial power of the United States shall be vested in one Supreme Court, and in such inferior courts as Congress may from time to time ordain and establish." [8] We find, also, in conformity with the system of checks and balances, so dear to the hearts of the framers, that the Constitution provides that the President shall possess the legislative veto power, and the right to pardon in certain cases, a judicial power; that the legislature possesses the judicial power of impeachment, and the power to judge the qualifications of its own members; the Senate, besides, participates with the executive in the appointment of civil officials and in the exercise of the treaty-making power; the courts, likewise, possess the power to establish rules of procedure which is essentially legislative, and the power to appoint certain officials, an executive power.

It is upon the doctrine of the separation of governmental powers that the courts have frequently based their refusal to decide questions which they deem to be political. But, in spite of the fact that the Supreme Court in *Luther* v. *Borden* invoked the doctrine to uphold its contention that it could not decide the question, which of two organizations

---

[5] *The Federalist*, ed., E. H. Scott, I, 266. See also William Bondy, *The Separation of Governmental Powers*, " Columbia University Studies in History, Economics and Public Law," V, no. 2; and John A. Fairlie, " The Separation of Powers," *Michigan Law Review*, XXI, 393.

[6] Art. 1, sec. 1.   [7] Art. 2, sec. 1.   [8] Art. 3, sec. 1.

was the *de jure* government of Rhode Island, it will be shown later that its refusal was founded on more practical grounds. This applies also to other cases to be discussed in subsequent chapters.

With this short and conventional statement of the nature of political questions and the reasons alleged for their existence, it seems only proper to consider the purposes and the method followed in the preparation of this study. It may be said immediately that this study is not concerned with " political questions " in the abstract, as " something considered in isolation from elements that accompany it in nature," [9] by which is meant that the term, except in a concrete and practical sense, for our purposes, at least, has no meaning. It is possible, if we enumerate all the things that can actually be accomplished by means of the doctrine, that we shall find in the consequences of its application the meaning of political questions. As a result, the writer has been led to propound two questions, the solutions of which he hopes to discover in a study of the cases. The first question is: What gives rise to the utilization of the concept? or, to put the question more precisely, what causes a jurist to place a particular problem in this category? Secondly, what are the consequences which result from the decision of a court to place a problem in the category of political questions? Perhaps it will be possible, from a consideration of the cases, to discover what prompts the courts consciously and purposely to anticipate these consequences. In other words, this work constitutes an experimental study of a particular problem—political questions as a category of the judicial thought process. There will not be overmuch concern with the " idea " of political questions, but more with the actual effect of the " idea." We all know, in a general way, the results of touching a lighted match to the fuse of a well-made firecracker; and in most cases it is obvious why a boy is prompted to ignite the fuse. What happens when a jurist labels a particular problem a political question, and why he does so, is what the writer attempts to discover in the course of this study.

---

[9] A. D. Richie, *Scientific Method,* p. 158.

CHAPTER II

Classification and Analysis of Some Cases Involving "Political Questions"

When we speak of the legal consequences attendant upon the disposition by a court of a problem as a political question, what do we mean? It is not intended immediately to answer this query with any degree of exactness, but, in general, it may be said that one of the legal consequences, and perhaps by far the most important, is to be found in the fact that once the court decides a question to be political, it then denies itself the privilege of deciding that question one way or another. What the court says in effect is this: We label this question, for instance, whether or not a war has been terminated, a political question, and by so doing, our attitude is that we cannot decide the question, but must depend upon the political departments, the executive and legislative departments of the government, to inform us, by act or word, of the proper decision to apply in the particular case. This would seem to be the legal effect of designating a problem a political question, and such effect will be found in practically all of the cases to be discussed.

I

The first instance [1] in which the Supreme Court availed itself of the opportunity to determine its own competence [2] concerning the clause of the Constitution guaranteeing to every state of the Union a republican form of government [3]

---

[1] "This is a new question in this court." *Luther* v. *Borden,* 7 How. 1, 35 (1849).

[2] This term is used advisedly, for it is possible that the Court might have construed the question as non-political.

[3] Article 4, section 4, of the Constitution of the United States provides that "The United States shall guarantee to every state in this Union a republican form of government, and shall protect each of them against invasion; and on application of the legislature, or of the executive, when the legislature cannot be convened, against domestic violence." The Constitution itself does not define the term "republican form of government," but it has, however, "always been

15

was *Luther* v. *Borden*,[4] decided in 1849. This case echoed what is commonly known as Dorr's Rebellion [5] of 1841. In that year, the old " Charter of Rhode Island and Providence Plantations," [6] granted the colony in 1663, was still in force. This instrument of government provided for only a limited suffrage, so limited, in fact, that with the development of democratic ideas attempts were made by those ineligible to vote to amend the Constitution in their favor; but to no avail. However, in 1841, the malcontents, taking the initiative, and not lacking in determination, by universal manhood suffrage, elected delegates to a constitutional convention. This extra-legal body, unsanctioned as it was by the

---

an accepted rule of construction that the technical and special terms used in the Constitution are to be given that meaning which they had at the time that instrument was framed." Westel W. Willoughby, *The Constitutional Law of the United States*, I, 215. Thus, a republican form of government has been defined as a " government by representatives chosen by the people; and it contrasts on one side with a democracy, in which the people or community as an organized whole wield sovereign powers of government, and on the other with the rule of one man, as king, emperor, czar, or sultan, or with one class of men, as an aristocracy. In strictness a republican government is by no means inconsistent with monarchical forms, for a king may be merely an hereditary or elective executive while the powers of legislation are left exclusively to a representative body freely chosen by the people. It is to be observed, however, that it is a republican *form* of government that is to be guaranteed; and in the light of the undoubted fact that by the Revolution it was expected and intended to throw off monarchical and aristocratic forms, there can be no question but that by a republican form of government was intended a government in which not only would the people's representatives make the laws, and their agents administer them, but the people would also, directly or indirectly, choose the executive." Thomas M. Cooley, *Principles of Constitutional Law*, pp. 247-248. Chief Justice Fuller, in the case of *Duncan* v. *McCall*, 139 U. S. 449 (1891), was led in the course of his opinion to define the term. He said: " The distinguishing feature of that form is the right of the people to choose their own officers for governmental administration, and to pass their own laws in virtue of the legislative power reposed in representative bodies, whose legitimate acts may be said to be those of the people themselves; but while the people are thus the source of political power, their governments, national and state, have been limited by written Constitutions, and they have themselves thereby set bounds to their own power, as against the sudden impulses of mere majorities."

    [4] 7 How. 1 (1849).
    [5] For a detailed account of this incident, see Arthur M. Mowry, *The Dorr War; or, the Constitutional Struggle in Rhode Island*.
    [6] Benjamin P. Poore, *The Federal and State Constitutions, Colonial Charters, and other Organic Laws of the United States*, II, 1595.

de jure government, proceeded to draft a constitution which, subsequently, was adopted by a majority of the adult male population of the state. Under this instrument, Thomas W. Dorr was elected governor. But the life of the new government was short. Dorr attempted to uphold what he deemed the lawful government by force of arms, but after a few skirmishes, the illegitimate constitution was abandoned.

The case of *Luther* v. *Borden* [7] which developed out of this incident, was an action of trespass [8] brought by Martin Luther, the plaintiff-in-error, against Luther Borden and others, for breaking and entering the plaintiff's house. The defendants maintained that, due to the insurrection described above, in which the position of the *de jure* government was threatened, martial law had been declared by competent authority; that the plaintiff had been involved in the insurrection, and that the defendants, as members of the militia in the service of the state, on the command of a superior officer, had broken into the house of Luther in order to arrest him. On the other hand, the plaintiff contended that previous to the alleged trespass the old government under which the defendants had acted "had been displaced and annulled by the people of Rhode Island," [9] and that he, the plaintiff, at the time was "engaged in supporting the lawful authority of the State, and the defendants themselves were in arms against it." [10] Thus, the very authority and existence of the *de jure* government was questioned, and the court was faced with the necessity of discovering which of the two governments was the lawful one.

But the Supreme Court in this case did not determine whether the charter government was still *de jure* in character, nor whether it was republican in form. These questions were held to be political questions and therefore not within the jurisdiction of the court. Chief Justice Taney, expressing the majority opinion, said:

---

[7] 7 How. 1.
[8] This case was heard in the federal courts since the validity of the government of Rhode Island was called into question under Art. 4, sec. 4, of the federal Constitution.
[9] 7 How. 35.   [10] *Ibid.*

Under this article [11] of the Constitution it rests with Congress to decide what government is the established one in a State. For as the United States guarantee to each State a republican government, Congress must necessarily decide what government is established in the State before it can determine whether it is republican or not. And when the senators and representatives of a State are admitted into the councils of the Union, the authority of the government under which they are appointed, as well as its republican character, is recognized by the proper constitutional authority. And its decision is binding on every other department of the government, and could not be questioned in a judicial tribunal.[12]

The court admitted, however, that " Congress was not called upon to decide the controversy " [13] since the Dorr Rebellion was of short duration and particularly since " no senators or representatives were elected under the authority of the government of which Mr. Dorr was the head." [14]

However, it is Congress in whose hands is left the determination of the " means proper to be adopted to fulfill this guarantee," [15] that is, the guarantee of a republican form of government. The power of such determination might have been placed in the courts, but this was not done. By act of February 28, 1795, it was provided that " in case of an insurrection in any State against the government thereof, it shall be lawful for the President of the United States, on application of the Legislature of such State or of the executive (when the Legislature cannot be convened), to call forth such number of the militia of any other State or States, as may be applied for, as he may judge sufficient to suppress such insurrection." [16]   And it is obvious, in order

---

[11] Art. 4, sec. 4.   [12] 7 How. 42.   [13] Ibid.

[14] Ibid.   The Constitution of the United States provides that each house of Congress shall determine the qualifications of its own members.   Suppose that under the Dorr Constitution of 1841 certain individuals had been elected to serve in Congress.   Suppose too, that the House had accepted the credentials of the representatives elected by the new faction, while the Senate recognized the Senators elected under the Charter government.   The Constitution does not anticipate such a situation.

[15] Ibid. 43.

[16] 1 Stat. L. 424.   It was decided in an earlier case, Martin v. Mott, 12 Wheat. 19 (1827), that the court could not question the decision of the President, acting under authority of this statute, to call forth the militia in order to repel invasion or suppress rebellion.   The court said: " We are all of opinion that the authority to decide whether the exigency has arisen, belongs exclusively to the President, and that his decision is conclusive upon all other persons."   Cf. Sterling v. Constantin, 278 U. S. 378 (1932).

that the President may act in accordance with the duty placed upon him by this statute, that he must first " determine what body of men constitute the Legislature, and who is the governor, before he can act." [17]

The Dorr Rebellion did not prompt the President to call out the militia. This was found to be unnecessary. But the President, upon application of the governor of the old government, did recognize him " as the executive power of the State, and took measures to call out the militia to support his authority if it should be found necessary "; and, continued Chief Justice Taney, " no court of the United States, with a knowledge of this decision, would have been justified in recognizing the opposing party as the lawful government." [18]

So, for the purpose of the court, the political departments had acted; they had decided which of the two contending governments was the lawful one. In the action of the President lay the decision that the old charter government was the *de jure* government. Now, the only remaining question was the legality or illegality of the alleged trespass by the defendants, and for the court this was simple of solution. " A State may," said Taney, " use its military power to put down an armed insurrection, too strong to be controlled by the civil authority. . . . And in that state of things the officers engaged in its (Rhode Island's) military service might lawfully arrest anyone, who . . . they had reasonable grounds to believe was engaged in the insurrection; and might order a house to be forcibly entered and searched. . . ." [19] And since Luther, in perpetrating the alleged trespass, had acted under the authority of the *de jure* government faced with insurrection, the decision is perhaps too obvious to recite.

A more recent case in which the Supreme Court was afforded the opportunity to express its opinion as to this question was *Pacific States Telephone Company* v. *The State of Oregon*,[20] decided in 1912. A more direct application of

---

[17] 7 How. 43.
[18] *Ibid.*, 44.

[19] *Ibid.*, 45-46.
[20] 223 U. S. 118 (1912).

the doctrine of political questions would be difficult to find.
The point at issue was whether a state has lost the characteristics of a republican form of government within the meaning of the guaranty clause of the Constitution because of
the adoption, by the state, of the initiative and referendum.
By resort to the initiative in 1906, a law taxing certain cor-
porations was submitted, voted on, and promulgated by the
governor of Oregon in 1907 as duly adopted. Under this
law, telephone and telegraph companies were taxed by what
was called an annual license, and penalties for non-conform-
ance were provided. The Pacific States Telephone Company
refused to make payment, maintaining that the adoption and
use of the initiative and referendum deprived the former
state government of its lawful character in the light of article 4, section 4, of the Constitution. All other contentions
of the defendant company were based on this; and the court,
holding that the whole case involved a political question,
dismissed it for want of jurisdiction.

In *Luther* v. *Borden* and the Oregon case it would seem
that the doctrine of political questions was applied conventionally. But if we consider another case, that of *Texas* v.
White,[21] we shall find that it holds a superficially anomalous
position, for here, in spite of the fact that the court held
itself bound by the action of the political departments, it
nevertheless *in effect* decided the question whether the government of Texas, subsequent to the termination of the Civil
War and prior to 1870, had been recognized by Congress.

Congress, by act of September 9, 1850, offered Texas, as
compensation for her claims connected with the settlement
of her boundaries and other disputes,[22] ten million dollars

---

[21] 7 Wall. 700 (1869).

[22] "The State of Texas cedes to the United States all her claim to
territory exterior to the limits and boundaries which she agrees to
establish by the first article of this agreement.

"The State of Texas relinquishes all claim upon the United States
for liability of the debts of Texas, and for compensation or indemnity
for the surrender to the United States of her ships, forts, arsenals,
custom-houses . . . and public buildings with their sites, which became
the property of the United States at the time of the annexation.

"The United States in consideration of said establishment of
boundaries, cession of claim to territory, and relinquishment of

iu five per centum bonds, each for the sum of one thousand dollars. This offer was accepted by the state,[23] and, subsequently, one-half of the bonds were delivered to the state, while the other half remained in the national treasury " to be issued to the holders of the Texas debt." [24]

The bonds were received on behalf of the state by the Comptroller of Public Accounts, under authority of an act of the legislature, which, besides granting that authority, provided that no bond should be available in the hands of any holder until endorsed by the governor of the state. With the outbreak of the rebellion, however, the revolutionary legislature of Texas promptly repealed [25] the act requiring the endorsement of the governor to validate the bonds, and on the same day made provision for the organization of a Military Board, composed of the governor, the comptroller, and treasurer, and authorized a majority of that board to provide for the defense of the state by means of any bonds in the state treasury, upon any account, to the extent of one million dollars. The defense intended by this act was to be made against the United States. Under this authority, the Military Board entered into an agreement [26] with G. W. White and others, who, in return for one hundred and thirty-five of the above-mentioned bonds, then in the state treasury,[27] agreed to deliver to the board certain quantities of cotton cards and medicines. Subsequently, one hundred and thirty-five of the bonds were delivered to White, none of which bore the signature of the governor.

With the close of the war,[28] Texas was without any or-

---

claims, will pay to the State of Texas the sum of ten millions of dollars in a stock bearing five per cent interest, and redeemable at the end of fourteen years, the interest payable half-yearly at the treasury of the United States." *Congressional Record*, 38th Cong., 1st sess., ch. xlix.

[23] November 25, 1850.

[24] William W. Pierson, " Texas *versus* White," *Southwestern Historical Quarterly*, XVIII, 344.

[25] January 11, 1862. [26] January 12, 1862.

[27] And for seventy-six more, at the time deposited with an English firm, Drooge & Co., London.

[28] See William A. Dunning, *Reconstruction, Political and Economic.* A lively account of the period immediately following the war is to be found in Claude Bowers, *The Tragic Era.*

ganized civil government recognized by the United States government. The President of the United States, therefore, by virtue of his military powers as commander-in-chief of the army and navy, instituted a provisional government and appointed a provisional governor. A new constitution was adopted, and, under it, a governor and other state and national officers were elected by the people. However, the duly elected senators and representatives to the national Congress were not granted their seats. And, when the Radicals assumed control in Congress, it was decreed that no legal governments existed in any of the previously rebellious states, which were thereupon grouped into five military districts, each under the supervision of a general appointed by the President.[29] Thus, each of the former Confederate states was reduced to a position of abject subordination to the national government, each lacking those qualities and characteristics indicative of a state as a member of the Union.

In 1868, Texas, claiming the above-mentioned bonds of the United States as her property, sought an injunction in the Supreme Court to restrain the defendants, White *et al.,* from receiving dividends from the national government. Texas also sought to compel the surrender of the bonds to the state.

The defendants maintained first, that sufficient authority had not been shown " for the prosecution of the suit in the name and on behalf of the State of Texas ";[30] and second, that since the state had severed her relations with the Union, her status was so altered as to render it incompetent to bring suit in the federal courts. The first contention was readily disproved by the evidence, the solicitors having been authorized by proper and lawful authorities to prosecute the suit.[31] The second allegation, as to the jurisdiction of the

---

[29] See Reconstruction Acts, March 2, 14 *Stat. L.* 428; March 23, 15 *Stat. L.* 2; July 19, 15 *Stat. L.* 30.

[30] 7 Wall. 719 (1869).

[31] "A letter of authority . . . has been produced, in which J. W. Throckmorton, elected Governor under the constitution adopted in 1866, and proceeding under an Act of the State Legislature relating to these bonds, expressly ratifies and confirms the action of the solicitors who filed the bill, and empowers them to prosecute this suit. . . ." *Ibid.,* 719.

court, received more attention, for if, said the court, "the State of Texas was not at the time of filing this bill, or is not now, one of the United States, we have no jurisdiction of this suit and it is our duty to dismiss it." [32]

Irrespective of secession and rebellion, when Texas was admitted to the Union, said Chase, "she entered into an indissoluble relation. All the obligations of perpetual union,[33] and all the guaranties of republican government in the Union, attached at once to the State. The Act which consummated her admission into the Union was something more than a compact; it was the incorporation of a new member into the political body. And it was final." [34] But, in order to sue in the Supreme Court, it was necessary that there be a state government "competent to represent the State in its relations with the National Government so far at least as the institution and prosecution of a suit is concerned." [35]

It will be remembered that at the end of the war the government of Texas was non-existent; that is, there was no government maintaining "constitutional relations with the Union." [36] Consequently, under article 4, section 4, of the Constitution, it was the duty of Congress to effect the institution of a republican form of government in the state. And from the guaranty clause was derived the authority for the reconstruction activities of the Federal government. But instead of reestablishing governments republican in form in the ex-Confederate states, the Radicals in Congress, under the domination of Thaddeus Stevens, passed the three Reconstruction Acts of 1867,[37] the first of which swept away the existing state governments [38] and grouped the hitherto rebellious states into five military districts "subject to the military authority of the United States," and made the adop-

---

[32] *Ibid.*

[33] "What can be indissoluble if a perpetual union, made more perfect, is not?" 7 Wall. 725.

[34] *Ibid.*, 726.   [36] *Ibid.*, 729.

[35] *Ibid.*, 726-727.   [37] See *supra*, p. 22, note 29.

[38] Except Tennessee. Tennessee was restored to her former relations with the National Government, and was again entitled to representation in Congress by act of Congress, July 24, 1866. 14 *Stat. L.* 364.

tion of Article 14 of the Constitution a prerequisite to the restitution of the states' rights and privileges. The second and the third merely supplemented the first. Thus, the provisional government, under the authority of which the bill in the case of *Texas* v. *White* was filed, was alleged to be illegal.

But the court held otherwise. Quoting the dictum laid down in *Luther* v. *Borden* that " Congress must necessarily decide what government is established in the State, before it can determine whether it is republican or not," [39] Chief Justice Chase held that Congress had decided the question with regard to Texas with the passage of the Reconstruction Acts. " It is important to observe," said Chase, " that these Acts themselves show that the governments, which had been established and had been in actual operation under executive direction, were recognized by Congress as provisional, as existing, and as capable of continuance," [40] with the result that the court held the suit to have been instituted by proper authority. As to the bondholders, it was held that their rights must be determined in the light of the objective for which the bonds were transferred, and that though Texas was legally a state of the Union during the secession period, it did not, *ipso facto,* follow that all the public acts of the state were valid acts; and, in particular, those acts passed in support of the insurrection were to be adjudged null and void.

It may be well at this point to examine the dissenting opinion of Mr. Justice Grier, who maintained, on the basis of a definition of a state as a member of the Union expressed by Chief Justice Marshall in the case of *Hepburn* v. *Ellzey*,[41] that Texas was not a state of the Union. Grier said:

Is Texas a State, now represented by members chosen by the people of that State and received on the floor of Congress? Has she two Senators to represent her as a State in the Senate of the United States? Has her voice been heard in the late election of the President? Is she not now held and governed as a conquered province by

---

[39] 7 How. 42.
[40] 7 Wall. 731.   [41] 2 Cranch 445, 452 (1805).

military force? The Act of Congress of March 28th, 1867,[42] declares
Texas to be a "Rebel State," and provides for its government until
a legal and republican State Government could be legally established.
It constituted Louisiana and Texas the 5th military district, and
made it subject, not to the civil authority, but to the "military
authorities of the United States." It is true [Justice Grier con-
tinued] that no organized rebellion now exists there, and the courts
of the United States now exercise jurisdiction over the people of that
province. But this is no test of the State's being in the Union;
Dakota is no State, and yet the courts of the United States administer justice there as they do in Texas. The Indian tribes, who are
governed by military force, cannot claim to be States of the Union.
Wherein does the condition of Texas differ from theirs? [43]

Furthermore, Justice Grier was of the opinion that Congress had decided that Texas was not a state. "I do not
consider myself bound," he said, "to express any opinion
judicially as to the constitutional right of Texas to exercise
the rights and privileges of a State of this Union, or the
power of Congress to govern her as a conquered province, to
subject her to military domination, and keep her in pupil-
age. I can only submit to the fact as decided by the political
position of the government; and I am not disposed to join
in any essay to prove Texas to be a State of this Union,
when Congress have decided that she is not." [44] If it be
admitted that Justice Grier's opinion is more realistic, and
from the point of view of logic, more satisfactory than the
opinion of the majority (and the majority justices must
have been cognizant of the facts as expressed by Grier), why,
then, did Chase resort to circumlocution and a doubtful
application of the doctrine of political questions?

Professor Field, in his article, "The Doctrine of Political
Questions in the Federal Courts," [45] concludes that "the
upshot of the decision in *Texas v. White* is merely this, that
a state does not need to have a republican form of government in order to maintain suit in the Supreme Court." [46]
For the purposes of this study, however, a more significant
conclusion may be drawn. Though Chase held that the

---

[42] Grier is evidently referring to the Act of March 2, 1867. 14
Stat. L. 428.

[43] 7 Wall. 738.

[44] *Ibid.*, 739.

[45] *Minnesota Law Review*, VIII, 485.

[46] *Ibid.*, 508.

political departments had acted in recognizing the provisional government of Texas as established, it is submitted here that such recognition as interpreted by Chase was never the intention of Congress. It is true, section 6 of the first Reconstruction Act provided that " any civil governments which may exist" in any of the Confederate states, " shall be deemed provisional only, and in all respects subject to the paramount authority of the United States at any time to abolish, modify, control, or supersede. . . ." [47] But it will be remembered that Justice Grier in his dissenting opinion was not disposed to " prove Texas to be a State of the Union, when Congress have decided that she is not "; [48] Congress—and it is the duty of the legislative department to decide what government is established in a state, and that in common constitutional parlance, this act of recognition is a political act and not within the jurisdiction of the courts—was opposed to the recognition of any of the provisional governments. The preamble of the first Reconstruction Act [49] specifically stated that " no legal State governments or adequate protection for life or property now exists in the rebel States," and that, " it is necessary that peace and good order should be enforced in said States until loyal and republican State governments can be legally established." [50] By this act the old Confederate states were divided into military districts, and " all interference under color of State authority with the exercise of military authority under this act, shall be null and void." [51] This act also enumerated the conditions upon which the old Confederate states should be entitled to representation in Congress.[52]

Furthermore, Texas was not readmitted into the Union until 1870, and this was done by act of Congress.[53] The preamble of the admitting act stated that the " people of Texas have framed and adopted a constitution of State government which is republican." [54]

---

[47] 14 *Stat. L.* 429.
[48] 7 Wall. 739.
[49] 14 *Stat. L.* 428.
[50] *Ibid.*

[51] *Ibid.*
[52] *Ibid.*, 429.
[53] 16 *Stat. L.* 80.
[54] *Ibid.*

In the light of the foregoing it does not seem unreasonable to conclude that, at the time of *Texas* v. *White,* the attitude of Congress was overlooked by Chase and the majority associates, and that it was not the Congress, but the Supreme Court, a non-political department, which had decided the political question. Such a conclusion, however, would be lacking in accuracy. Legally, the Supreme Court did not decide the political question. Mr. Justice Grier discovered the attitude of Congress with regard to the political question in the obvious tenor of the Reconstruction Acts; Chief Justice Chase found the attitude of Congress in the Reconstruction Acts, too, but only as these acts indicated that the new governments of the former Confederate states had been " recognized by Congress as provisional, as existing, and as capable of continuance." [55] In as much as Chief Justice Chase and the majority associates could have followed Grier, it is evident that a choice of attitudes (from the point of view of the court) was presented to the court for its consideration. And in so far as the answer to the political question involved a choice, the question became, in part, a judicial question.

It cannot be doubted that Chase knew the view of Congress as to the provisional governments; nor can it be doubted that he repudiated the general intention of the Congress with regard to these governments. Why the majority did this will be discussed in a later chapter. On other than legal grounds this action is, perhaps, more readily understood.

II

Another question, relative to the internal policy of the Federal government, and deemed by the courts to be political, is the legal status of Indian tribes. With the formulation and acceptance of the Constitution by the thirteen original states, the policy of Europe, and later the states, toward the Indian was perpetuated. A possessory right to the soil, on which the Indians wandered, hunted and established occa-

---

[55] 7 Wall. 731.

sional settlements, was recognized by the white men; but, since it was claimed, and claimed with superior force, that the ultimate title to the land, by right of discovery, lay in the hands of the whites,[56] the possessory rights of the Indians were subordinate in character. The Indian tribes were forbidden to sell or transfer their lands to other peoples or foreign nations without the approval of the government of the United States. If the government wished to purchase land from the Indians, a treaty was the usual means of doing so. Furthermore, the national government recognized no right in private persons to make such a purchase by treaty or in any other manner. " They [the Indians] were, and always have been, regarded as having a semi-independent position when they preserved their tribal relationship; not as States, not as Nations, not as possessed of the full attributes of sovereignty, but as a separate people, with the power of regulating their internal and social relations, and thus far not brought under the laws of the Union or of the State within whose limits they resided." [57]   It is obvious that in the constitutional system of the United States the tribal Indian was neither fish nor fowl, being neither a foreigner nor a domestic citizen, dependent upon the national government for what independence he might enjoy. To quote a modern publicist, " these rights have been at all times subject to withdrawal without the Indians' consent." [58]   An instance of this was the passage of a law by Congress providing that " no Indian nation or tribe within the territory of the United States shall be acknowledged or recognized as an independent nation, tribe or power with whom the United States may contract by treaty," [59] a law which was unsolicited by the Indians themselves.[60]

The power of the national government to control the des-

---

[56] See *Holden* v. *Joy*, 17 Wall. 211 (1872).
[57] *United States* v. *Kagama*, 118 U. S. 375 (1886).
[58] Willoughby, I, 388.
[59] 16 *Stat. L.* 566 (March 3, 1871).
[60] For further discussion as to the relation of the Indian to the national government, see Willoughby, I, 379; G. F. Canfield, " The Legal Position of the Indian," *American Law Review*, XV, 21; A. H. Snow, *The Question of the Aborigines*.

tinies of the tribal Indian has been derived from four sources: the power to regulate commerce, the power to dispose of and make all needful rules and regulations respecting the territories of the United States, the power to make treaties and, finally, the vague power over the Indians as "wards" of the nation.

The Constitution provides that Congress shall have power "to regulate commerce with foreign nations, and among the several States, and with the Indian Tribes." [61]   This clause does not affect the non-tribal Indian.[62]   However, the clause has been broadly construed, particularly since it has been supplemented by what may be called a second source of federal control which, in effect, amounts to a general jurisdiction over the Indians as wards of the nation.[63]

There is no provision in the Constitution which gives to Congress control over the Indians as "wards" of the nation, and on strictly legal grounds such control might be deemed unconstitutional.[64]   Yet much use has been made of the concept.   In one case, the court said:

> These Indian Tribes *are* the wards of the Nation.   They are communities *dependent* on the United States; dependent largely for their daily food; dependent for their political rights.   They owe no allegiance to the States, and receive from them no protection. . . . From their very weakness and helplessness, so largely due to the course of dealing of the Federal Government with them and the treaties in which it has been promised, there arises the duty of protection, and with it the power.   This has always been recognized by the Executive and by Congress, and by this court whenever the question has arisen.[65]

And as Professor Field has said, though from the point of view of constitutional law the doctrine may seem irregular,

---

[61] Art. 1, sec. 8, cl. 3.

[62] "Prior to the adoption of the Constitution, the Indian tribes had been treated as independent or quasi-independent political bodies, and it would appear that the framers of the Constitution had taken it for granted that, after the inauguration of the new government, this would continue to be their status and therefore that they were to be dealt with by the Federal Government by means of treaties and under the treaty-making powers of the Federal Government.   And this, in fact was the procedure followed."   Willoughby, I, 381.

[63] See *United States* v. *Kagama*, 118 U. S. 375 (1886).

[64] See Willoughby, I, 390.

[65] *United States* v. *Kagama*, 118 U. S. 383-384.

" the language which has been used by the court at times would seem to warrant the belief that legislation relating to Indians would be upheld on this ground if other sources failed." [66]

The Constitution provides that " the Congress shall have power to dispose of and make all needful rules and regulations respecting the territory or other property belonging to the United States; and nothing in this Constitution shall be so construed as to prejudice any claims of the United States, or of any particular state." [67]   As a third source of power of the national government to control tribal Indians this provision of the Constitution was once more important than it is at present,[68] but with the gradual development of territories into states the effect of this provision obviously was limited to the reservation.

Previous to 1871, the power of the President to deal with the Indian tribes lay in his power to make treaties.   Before and after the establishment of the Union in 1789, it had been customary to negotiate with the Indians by means of treaties, and the power of the President to make treaties was construed to entitle him to make treaties with the Indian tribes.[69]   However, on March 3, 1871, an act [70] was passed by Congress providing that no tribe within the territory of the United States should be recognized as an independent nation with which the Federal government could contract by treaty.   But, as Canfield has so well said:

> The object of this statute was not to destroy the tribes as distinct communities, but simply to deprive the President of his treaty-making power; for it is to be noticed that it says not that no Indian tribe shall be recognized as a *nation or tribe,* but that no Indian tribe shall be recognized as a *nation or tribe capable of contracting with us by treaty,* and then it provides specially that existing

---

[66] Field, p. 504.

[67] Art. 4, sec. 3, cl. 2.

[68] See *Dorr* v. *United States,* 195 U. S. 138 (1904) ; *Murphy* v. *Ramsey,* 114 U. S. 15 (1885) ; *United States* v. *Kagama,* 118 U. S. 375 (1886) ; *Camfield* v. *United States,* 167 U. S. 518 (1897) ; *Clinton* v. *Englebrecht,* 13 Wall. 434 (1872).

[69] *United States* v. *Forty-Three Gallons of Whiskey,* 93 U. S. 188 (1876) ; *Holden* v. *Joy,* 17 Wall. 211 (1872) ; *Lone Wolf* v. *Hitchcock,* 187 U. S. 553 (1903) ; *Conley* v. *Ballinger,* 216 U. S. 84 (1910).

[70] 16 *Stat. L.* 566.

treaties shall not be invalidated or impaired. If the tribes were destroyed as tribes, how could the treaties with them continue to have force? And this is the interpretation which is alone consistent with the action of Congress and the decisions of the courts, for they have both continued to recognize the Indian tribes as a distinct, quasi-sovereign people. . . . Such being the object of the statute . . . it follows that the Indians will be henceforth solely under the power of Congress, the President no longer having power to enter into treaties with them.[71]

Thus, it is evident that the legal supremacy of the Federal government over the Indians in the tribal state is a fact without question, and as long as the Indians remain within the tribe [72] their rights and privileges are determined by the government of the United States; furthermore, it must be remembered that it is not the states, nor is it the courts, that determine the legal status of the Indian, or group of Indians, but a political department of the Federal government.

An early case involving the legal status of the Indian tribe was *The Cherokee Nation* v. *The State of Georgia*,[73] decided in 1831. Before discussing this controversy, however, and in order to see the case in its proper perspective, an account of its background is necessary.

The Cherokee Indians of Georgia, in 1827, drew up a constitution,[74] fashioned a government, following that of the United States, and declared themselves a sovereign nation. Toward this action, the Georgia legislature responded in no uncertain terms. Resolutions were passed to the effect that " all the lands, appropriated and unappropriated, which lie within the conventional limits of Georgia belong to her absolutely; that the title is in her; that the Indians are tenants at her will . . . and that Georgia has the right to extend her authority and her laws over her whole territory and to coerce obedience to them from all descriptions of people, be they white, red, or black, who may reside within her limits." [75]

---

[71] *American Law Review*, XV, 24.

[72] However, see Lewis Meriam and Associates, *The Problem of Indian Administration*, pp. 743-811.

[73] 5 Peters 1 (1831).

[74] For text of the Cherokee constitution, see *House Document*, No. 91, 23d Cong., 2d sess.

[75] *Acts of Georgia General Assembly, 1827*, p. 249. Quoted from Ulrich B. Phillips, " Georgia and State Rights," *Annual Report of the American Historical Association, 1901*, II, 72.

The state then proceeded to enact laws confiscating the Indian lands and dividing them into counties. Appeal was made by the Cherokees to President Jackson; but from this quarter no assistance was forthcoming. Jackson, in this instance a believer in State Rights, maintained that Georgia had complete authority over the Indians.[76]

At this time gold was discovered in the Indian country,[77] and hordes of adventurers congregated in the mining districts. In the face of this, the Georgia legislature passed laws forbidding the Cherokees to hold courts or legislative assemblies. A state guard was stationed about the mines to assure protection and enforce the laws of Georgia. Furthermore, white persons found within the Indian country without license from the governor were to receive long prison sentences. When the Georgia legislature completed its work, " the sovereignty and jurisdiction " [78] of the Cherokee state was non-existent. As a consequence the Cherokees applied to the Supreme Court for an injunction to restrain the State of Georgia from executing these acts. The injunction prayed for by the plaintiffs, however, was denied on the ground that the Cherokee Nation was not a foreign nation or state in the sense of the term as used in that provision of the Constitution extending the federal judicial power to controversies " between a State or the citizens thereof, and foreign States, citizens or subjects," [79] and that therefore, the court had no jurisdiction.

However, Marshall expressed the opinion, *obiter* to be sure, but significant since it was relied upon by the court in *Georgia* v. *Stanton*,[80] that

---

[76] " I informed the Indians inhabiting parts of Georgia and Alabama that their attempt to establish an independent government would not be countenanced by the Executive of the United States." From Jackson's 1st annual message. J. D. Richardson, ed., *Messages and Papers of the Presidents*, III, 1021.

[77] Phillips, p. 72.

[78] Cherokee Constitution (1827), Art. 1, sec. 2, *H. Doc.*, no. 91, 23d Cong., 2d sess.

[79] Art. 3, sec. 2, cl. 1.

[80] 6 Wall. 50 (1867). The Supreme Court in this case dismissed for want of jurisdiction a bill seeking to restrain the Secretary of War, General Grant, and General Pope, from enforcing the Recon-

A serious additional objection exists to the jurisdiction of the court. Is the matter of the bill the proper subject for judicial inquiry and decision? It seeks to restrain a State from the forcible exercise of legislative power over a neighboring people asserting their independence, their right which the State denies. On several of the matters alleged in the bill, for example on the laws making it criminal to exercise the usual powers of self-government in their own country by the Cherokee Nation, this court cannot interpose, at least in the form in which those matters are presented. That part of the bill which respects the land occupied by the Indians and prays the aid of the court to protect their possession may be more doubtful. The mere question of right might be decided by this court in a proper case with proper parties. But the court is asked to do more than decide on the title. The bill requires us to control the legislature of Georgia, and to restrain the exertion of its physical force. The propriety of such an interposition by the court may well be questioned. It savors too much of the exercise of political power to be within the proper province of the judicial department. But the opinion on the point respecting parties makes it unnecessary to decide this question.[81]

Thus, even had the parties been proper litigants, the case would hardly have been decided, because the question involved was political.

It would seem in the later cases involving the legal status of the Indian tribes that recourse by the courts to the category of political questions has tended to uphold and strengthen the power of Congress over the Indian and to minimize that of the states. For example, the question arose

---

struction Acts in Georgia. " In looking into it," said Mr. Justice Nelson, " it will be seen that we are called upon to restrain the defendants, who represent the executive authority of the government, from carrying into execution certain acts of Congress, inasmuch as such execution would annul, and totally abolish the existing state government of Georgia . . . in other words, would overthrow and destroy the corporate existence of the state. . . . That these matters, both as stated in the body of the bill, and in the prayers for relief, call for the judgment of the court upon political questions, and, upon rights, not of persons or property, but of a political character, will hardly be denied." 6 Wall. 76-77. In *Mississippi* v. *Johnson*, 4 Wall. 475 (1867), the Supreme Court was requested to restrain the executive from applying the Reconstruction Acts to the State of Mississippi. Mr. Chief Justice Chase, with reference to the relations of the three departments of government, said: " The impropriety of such interference will be clearly seen upon consideration of its possible consequences. Suppose the bill filed and the injunction prayed for allowed. If the President refuse obedience, it is needless to observe that the court is without power to enforce its process." 4 Wall. 500-501.

[81] 5 Pet. 20 (1831).

in *United States* v. *Holliday* [82] whether an Indian to whom
liquor was sold by the defendant, was to be considered as
under the charge of an Indian agent. The defendant maintained that, by the treaty of August 2, 1855,[83] the tribe in
question had been dissolved. The court held, however, to
the view that this treaty required the tribal relation to continue, for certain purposes, until 1865. " The facts in the
case . . . show distinctly," said Justice Miller, " ' that the
Secretary of the Interior and the Commissioner of Indian
Affairs have decided that it is necessary, in order to carry
into effect the provisions of said treaty, that the tribal organization should be preserved.' In reference to all matters
of this kind, it is the rule of this court to follow the action
of the executive and other political departments of the government, whose more special duty it is to determine such
affairs. If by them those Indians are recognized as a tribe,
this court must do the same. If they are a tribe of Indians,
then, by the Constitution of the United States, they are
placed, for certain purposes, within the control of the laws
of Congress." [84]   And, continued Justice Miller, " this control extends . . . to the subject of regulating the liquor
traffic with them." [85]   As a result, Holliday was deemed liable for the offence of violating the act of 1862 [86] which provided that " if any person shall sell, exchange . . . or dispose of any spiritous liquor or wine to any Indian under the
charge of any Indian superintendent or Indian agent appointed by the United States . . . such person shall be im-
prisoned for a period not exceeding two years, and shall be
fined not more than three hundred dollars." [87]

Again, in the case of the Kansas Indians,[88] the question
raised was whether or not lands belonging to the Shawnee
Indians, residing in Kansas, were taxable by the state. This,
said the court, was dependent upon the legal status of the

---

[82] 3 Wall. 407 (1866).
[83] 11 *Stat. L.* 633.
[84] 3 Wall. 419.
[85] *Ibid.*
[86] 12 *Stat. L.* 338.
[87] *Ibid.*, 339.
[88] *Charles Blue Jacket* v. *Commissioners of Johnson County,* 5
Wall. 737 (1867).

tribe. Expressing the opinion of the court, Mr. Justice Davis said: " the action of the Political Department of the Government settles beyond controversy, that the Shawnees are as yet a distinct people, with a perfect tribal organization. Within a very recent period their head men negotiated a treaty with the United States [89]. . . and they are under the charge of an agent who constantly resides with them. While the General Government has a superintending care over their interests, and continues to treat with them as a nation, the State of Kansas is estopped from denying their title to it." [90]

In the opinion of the court in the case of *United States* v. *Sandoval*,[91] involving the introduction of intoxicating beverages into the Indian country, Mr. Justice Van Devanter, quoting from the case of *Marchie Tiger* v. *Western Improvement Company*,[92] said: " It may be taken as the settled doctrine of this court that Congress, in pursuance of the long-established policy of the government, has a right to determine for itself when the guardianship which has been maintained over the Indian shall cease. It is for that body, and not the courts, to determine when the true interests of the Indian require his release from such condition of tutelage." [93] But, said Justice Van Devanter, " it is not meant . . . that Congress may bring a community or body of people within the range of this power by arbitrarily calling them an Indian tribe, but only that in respect of distinctly Indian communities the questions whether, to what extent, and for what time they shall be recognized and dealt with as dependent tribes requiring the guardianship and protection of the

---

[89] This treaty, according to the opinion, was not ratified. 5 Wall. 757.

[90] 5 Wall. 756-757. See also, *Holden* v. *Joy*, 17 Wall. 211 (1872), " The Acts of our Government, both in the executive and legislative departments, plainly recognize such Tribes or Nations as States; and the courts of the United States are bound by those Acts." It must be remembered, however, that the term ' state ' in reference to an Indian tribe does not mean a state as that term is used in the Constitution.

[91] 231 U. S. 28 (1913)

[92] 221 U. S. 286 (1911).

[93] 231 U. S. 46.

United States [94] are to be determined by Congress, and not by the courts." [95]   Thus, Justice Van Devanter gave expression to the circumscribing power of the court with respect to the exercise of a political power.   It is within the power of Congress to label the inhabitants of an Indian community a tribe and assume control over them, but there the power ceases.   It would seem that were Congress to denominate a community of white people, or black, a tribe, and proceed to exercise control over them as a tribe, the court would object and declare such action unconstitutional.   The fact that a tribe or community of Indians *are Indians* establishes the jurisdiction of Congress.

III

These cases, so far as concerns those problems considered by the Supreme Court to be political questions, deal primarily with the internal policy and relations of the United States.   There is, however, another and larger group of questions which concern the relations of the United States with foreign countries.   Such questions, for example, are those of the commencement and termination of war,[96] jurisdiction over territory, and the interpretation of treaties.

It has been said that the " date at which a war begins is a political question." [97]   For instance, the war with Spain (1898) left in its wake no difficulty in the minds of jurists as to its commencement.   On April 20, 1898, President McKinley approved a joint resolution of Congress which was in the nature of an ultimatum.   This resolution declared (1) " that ' the people of Cuba are and of right ought to be, free and independent; ' (2) that it was the duty of the United States to demand, and that the United States did thereby demand, that Spain at once relinquish her authority and government in Cuba and withdraw her land and naval

---

[94] See *United States* v. *Nice*, 241 U. S. 591 (1916).

[95] 231 U. S. 46.

[96] It may be said that the most interesting application of the doctrine of political questions as far as it concerns the commencement and termination of war is to be found in those cases arising out of the American Civil War.

[97] Field, p. 490.

forces from the island and its waters; (3) that the President was directed and empowered to use the land and naval forces of the United States . . . ; and (4) that the United States disclaimed any disposition or intention to exercise sovereignty, jurisdiction, or control over the island except for the pacification thereof. . . ." [98] The following day the American Minister at Madrid " received from the Spanish Government a note, in which it was stated that the joint resolution was considered as an obvious declaration of war, and that all diplomatic relations consequently were severed." [99] A few days later,[100] by an act of Congress approved by the President, " war was declared to have existed since April 21, inclusive. . . ." [101]

Thus, in the case of the *Pedro*,[102] the court merely turned to the political departments to find the time of the beginning of the war writ large in an act of Congress. " And by the act of Congress of April 25," said the court, " it was declared that war had existed since the 21st day of April." [103]

Again, on the recommendation [104] of the President, Congress, on April 6, 1917, declared a state of war existed between Germany and the United States: " Whereas the Imperial German Government has committed repeated acts of war against the Government and the people of the United States: Therefore be it *Resolved by the Senate* and *House of Representatives of the United States of America in Congress assembled,* That the state of war between the United States and the Imperial German Government which has thus been thrust upon the United States is hereby formally declared. . . ." [105] So specific a declaration by Congress precludes all controversy.

---

[98] John B. Moore, *Digest of International Law,* VII, 170.
[99] *Ibid.*
[100] April 25, 1898.
[101] Moore, VII, 170-171.
[102] 175 U. S. 354 (1899).
[103] *Ibid.*, 363. See also the *Buena Ventura,* 175 U. S. 384 (1899); and the *Panama,* 176 U. S. 535 (1900).
[104] *Cong. Rec.,* 65th Cong., Special sess., p. 3.
[105] 40 *Stat. L.* (Part I) p. 1.

These instances are simple. Congress, possessing the power to declare war,[106] had acted; it had in the cases of the Spanish-American War and the World War specified the dates of commencement, and for the courts the decision of Congress was final. But not to hasten conclusions, it may be advantageous to look further afield.

It is admitted that when hostilities are ushered in by a written declaration, the time of the commencement of a war presents no difficulties to the courts; but when hostilities are begun without proclamation or communication of any sort, as in the case of the American Civil War, the difficulties are manifest. Previous to, and following, the suppression of the Rebellion, the Supreme Court, and other federal and state courts, were faced with innumerable controversies, acceptable solutions of which depended, in part at least, upon a determination of the time of the commencement of the struggle. According to the rule that the time of the beginning of a war is a political question, it might be logically concluded that, in cases arising out of the Civil War, the courts themselves did not fix the date of commencement; that, instead, the courts looked to the political departments for a solution. It is maintained here, however, that though the courts did look to the political departments for a time at which to set the date of the commencement of hostilities, the final determination of that date resolved itself partly into a judicial question. The political departments by act or word in several instances gave evidence of hostilities, but did not specify any one of these instances as marking the commencement of the war. In so far as the judiciary determined which one of these instances marked the beginning of the war, the determination of that date became, in part, a judicial question.

A decision as to the commencement and termination of the Civil War was made in the case of the *Protector*.[107] The issue was whether an appeal from a decree of the United States Circuit Court for Louisiana should be allowed, a mo-

---

[106] Art. 1, sec. 8, cl. 11.   [107] 12 Wall. 700 (1871).

tion having been brought from the United States Circuit Court for the Southern District of Alabama that the appeal be dismissed. In view of the law, appeals had to be presented within five years from the date of the decree complained of. The decree in this case was given April 5, 1861, and the appeal taken ten years later, May 17, 1871. And, since the statute of limitations did not apply during the Civil War, it was necessary that the period of the war be determined in order to ascertain the time to be deducted in estimating the amount of time that had elapsed. "It is necessary, therefore," said Chief Justice Chase, "to refer to some public act of the political departments of the government to fix the dates; and for obvious reasons, those of the Executive Department, which may be, and, in fact, was, at the commencement of hostilities, obliged to act during the recess of Congress, must be taken. The proclamation of intended blockade by the President may, therefore, be assumed as marking the first of these dates. . . ." [108] However, since the war did not begin at the same time in all the states, for the purposes of the court, two proclamations were accepted as indicative of the commencement of the war. These were the proclamations of April 19,[109] and April 27, 1861.[110] The former was taken to have begun the war between the Union and South Carolina, Georgia, Alabama, Florida, Mississippi, Louisiana and Texas; the latter, between the Union and North Carolina and Virginia.[111] The termination of the conflict was likewise found in two proclamations of the President.

So there were two Proclamations declaring that the war had closed; the first, issued April 2, 1866,[112] embraces the States of Virginia, North Carolina, South Carolina, Georgia, Florida, Mississippi, Tennessee, Alabama, Louisiana and Arkansas; and the second, issued on the 20th of August, 1866,[113] embracing the state of Texas.[114]

---

[108] *Ibid.*, 702.   [109] 12 *Stat. L.* 1258.   [110] 12 *Stat. L.* 1259.

[111] It is interesting to note that neither of these proclamations included Tennessee and Arkansas. The first proclamation declaring a state of war to exist in these States was that of August 16, 1861, 12 *Stat. L.* 1262. See *House Report*, no. 262, 43d Cong., 1st sess., pp. 77-78.

[112] 14 *Stat. L.* 811.   [113] *Ibid.*, 814.   [114] 12 Wall. 701.

Since more than five years had elapsed, the appeal was dismissed.

Now, the Constitution of the United States specifically provides that "Congress shall have power . . . to declare war,"[115] and, in the case of the Civil War, Congress, on July 13, 1861, recognized that a state of war existed.[116] And it was this Act that Justice Nelson,[117] in his dissenting opinion in the *Prize Cases*,[118] held to be indicative of the beginning of the war. In order to "constitute a civil war," said Justice Nelson, "before it can exist, in contemplation of law, it must be recognized or declared by the sovereign power of the State, and which sovereign power by our Constitution is lodged in the Congress of the United States—civil war, therefore, under our system of government, can exist only by an Act of Congress, which requires the assent of two of the great departments of the government, the Executive and Legislative. . . . Congress alone can determine whether war exists or should be declared. . . ."[119] Nelson was of the opinion that "no civil war existed between this Government and the States in insurrection till recognized by the Act of Congress 13th July 1861."[120] Nelson's construction of the Constitution is viewed with approval by a modern publicist:

It seems to have been a very questionable construction of the Constitution to hold that, in the case of a civil struggle, the President has the power, upon his own judgment, to affix to it the character of a public war, and thus to bring into existence all the many legal conditions which that status imports. That he should have full power to use all the forces of the nation to put down resistance to the execution of the Federal laws there can be no question, but it would seem that the explicit declaration of the Constitution that to Congress belongs the power to declare war necessarily excludes from the executive sphere of authority the power to pronounce that public war exists.[121]

However, a satisfactory interpretation of the majority opinion in the *Prize Cases* is not to be found in rules of

---

[115] Art. 1, sec. 8, cl. 11.   [116] 12 *Stat. L.* 1258.
[117] Taney, Catron and Clifford concurred in this dissent.
[118] 2 Black 635 (1862).
[119] *Ibid.*, 690.   [120] *Ibid.*, 698.
[121] Willoughby, III, 1559. See also James G. Randall, *Constitutional Problems under Lincoln*, pp. 52 ff.

law. The problem that presented itself to the court in the *Prize Cases* was how to apply the rules of international and prize law to neutrals who violated the blockade established by the Union government. The government had proceeded on the theory that the war was no more than an insurrection, and that two belligerent parties did not exist. The Secretary of State, Seward, to complicate matters further, in the two proclamations of blockade, maintained that no " war " existed, and the government itself protested vigorously against the recognition of the Confederacy as a belligerent by foreign governments. Had the court in the *Prize Cases* held that the rules of international law did not apply, the Union blockade would legally have been rendered ineffective.[122]

In giving the opinion of the majority, Justice Grier said: " It is not necessary, to constitute war, that both parties should be acknowledged as independent nations or sovereign States. A war may exist where one of the belligerents claims sovereign rights as against the other [123]. . . and

---

[122] For the substance of this paragraph, the writer is indebted to Charles Warren, *The Supreme Court in United States History*, III, 103-104. The Government's counsel in the *Prize Cases*, R. H. Dana, wrote: " These causes present our Constitution in a new and peculiar light. In all States but ours, now existing or that have ever existed, the function of the Judiciary is to interpret the acts of the Government. In ours, it is to decide their legality. The Government is carrying on a war. It is exerting all the powers of war. Yet the claimants of the captured vessels not only seek to save their vessels by denying that they are liable to capture but deny the right of the Government to exercise war power,—deny that this can be, in point of law, a war. So the Judiciary is actually, after a war of twenty-three months' duration, to decide whether the Government has the legal capacity to exert these war powers. . . . Contemplate, my dear sir, the possibility of a Supreme Court, deciding that this blockade is illegal! What a position it would put us in before the world whose commerce we have been illegally prohibiting, whom we have unlawfully subjected to a cotton famine, and domestic dangers and distress for two years! It would end the war, and how it would leave us with neutral powers, it is fearful to contemplate! Yet such an event is legally possible—I do not think it probable, hardly possible, in fact. But last year, I think there was danger of such a result, when the blockade was new and before the three new judges were appointed. The bare contemplation of such a possibility makes us pause in our boastful assertion that our written Constitution is clearly the best adapted to all exigencies, the last, best gift to man." Quoted in Warren, III, 104.
[123] 2 Black 666 (1862).

whether the hostile party be a foreign invader, or State organized in rebellion, it is none the less a war, although the declaration of it be ' unilateral.' . . .[124] The proclamation of blockade is, itself, official and conclusive evidence to the court that a state of war existed. . . ."[125]   And Justice Grier, in anticipation of the criticism that behind these two proclamations lay no legislative sanction, cited the Act of Congress of August 6, 1861, which provided that " all the acts, proclamations, and orders of the President of the United States after the fourth of March, eighteen hundred and sixty-one, respecting the army and navy of the United States, and calling out or relating to the militia or volunteers from the States, are hereby approved and in all respects legalized and made valid. . . ."[126]   Thus, it was held by the court, that the establishment of the blockade was within the lawful power of the President.   Had the minority opinion been the opinion of the majority, then the United States Government had been engaged in illegal acts on a large scale.   As it was, the Government barely escaped a crushing defeat.[127]   It must be remembered, however, that the court in the *Prize Cases* held that the President in proclaiming the blockades did not create a war, but merely took measures to protect the United States in a war thrust upon the government.   Furthermore, the President did not specify the dates of the blockade proclamations as marking the beginning of the war.

Even if the acts of the President were validated and legalized by the Act of August 6, that act did not in any way indicate the time of the commencement of the war.   It included, among other acts, the call for the militia,[128] which, in the light of its purposes, might have been deemed, in retrospect, an act of war.   " Whereas the laws of the United States," the proclamation ran, " have been, for some time

---

[124] *Ibid.*, 668.   [125] *Ibid.*, 670.
[126] 12 *Stat. L.* 326. " The objection made to this act of ratification," said Grier, " that it is *ex post facto* and therefore unconstitutional and void, might possibly have some weight on the trial of an indictment in a criminal court.   But precedents from that source cannot be received as authoritative in a tribunal administering public and international law."   2 Black 671.
[127] See Warren, III, 102 ff.   [128] 12 *Stat. L.* 1258.

past, and now are opposed, and the execution thereof obstructed, in the States of South Carolina, Georgia, Alabama, Florida, Mississippi, Louisiana and Texas, by combinations too powerful to be suppressed by the ordinary course of judicial proceedings, or by the powers vested in the marshals by law: Now, therefore, I, Abraham Lincoln, President of the United States, in virtue of the power in me vested by the Constitution . . . do call forth, the militia . . . in order to suppress said combinations. . . ."[129]   This proclamation, calling for the militia, was ignored by the court in the case of the *Protector*. Furthermore, the court, in defining the period of the war, disregarded the few days intervening between the struggle at Fort Sumter and the President's proclamations of blockade. Yet, it is interesting to note, in the treaty of Washington,[130] pertaining to certain war-time claims against Great Britain, the commencement of the war was set at April 13, 1861.

Out of this confusion the way seems difficult. Congress has the power to declare war, and, though Congress did not formally declare war against the seceded states, it did, on July 13, 1861, formally recognize, for the first time, the existence of a state of war. Congress, a political department, had acted, and in both the *Prize Cases* and the case of the *Protector,* this action of Congress was ignored. The acts of the President were legalized by act of Congress, but this act did not specify the date of the beginning of the war. It, therefore, seems reasonable to conclude that the Supreme Court itself, in part, at least, determined when the war began. The Executive presented certain acts, such as the call for the militia and the two proclamations of blockade, which were legalized by act of Congress; by act of Congress a state of war was recognized; and it is submitted that the Supreme Court could have chosen any one of these acts as indicating the beginning of the war, since Congress itself had not specified the date. Nor is it unreasonable to conclude, therefore,

---

[129] *Ibid.*
[130] *Treaties and Conventions Concluded between the United States and other Powers,* comp., John H. Haswell, 478 (484). (Hereafter cited as *Treaties and Conventions.*)

that though in general the time of the beginning of a war is a political question, when Congress fails to determine that time, the question becomes, in part, judicial.

The question remains, why did the court, in the case of the *Protector,* in defining the duration of the war, choose an act of the President rather than an act of Congress as indicative of the commencement of the war. It may be said that the court did so in order to avoid certain consequences deemed by them undesirable. In the *Prize Cases,* the blockade had been declared legal in view of the fact that a state of war [131] existed. Suppose that the court, in the case of the *Protector,* had declared that the Act of Congress of July 13, 1861, marked the beginning of the war. Then, according to this decision, as far as concerned foreign states, no war in the legal sense existed prior to July 13, with the result that all of the President's acts, including the two proclamations of blockade, were illegal, and the decision of the court in the *Prize Cases* an incorrect one. Such a decision, it is maintained here, and not unreasonably it is thought, would possibly have necessitated a certain readjustment on the part of the court, and the rehearing of cases incorrectly decided; the resultant confusion of such a decision, not only at home, but abroad as well, was what the court wished to avoid. The confusion is minimized when this case is approached from the point of view of the purposes of the court.

As to the termination of war, it may be said that war has usually ended [132] in one of three ways: the subjugation of one of the belligerents by the other; [133] the cessation of hostilities without treaty or agreement; [134] and, finally, by formal treaty. The treaty has been most often resorted to,

[131] A state of war has been defined as an " armed contest between two states or parts of the same state conducted by regularly organized military bodies and having an avowed political object in view. War may exist where no battle has been or is being fought, as well as when war has not been declared nor belligerency recognized." Edwin M. Borchard, *The Diplomatic Protection of Citizens Abroad,* pp. 248-249.

[132] See Coleman Phillipson, *Termination of War and Treaties of Peace.*

[133] War between Great Britain and South African Republic, 1902.

[134] See Moore, VII, 336-337.

since, with the conclusion of hostilities there arise new problems,[135] new situations, complex and evasive of solution, which are adjusted only by means of a written document setting forth the characteristics of the altered relationship, if alteration there be, for the benefit of the hitherto hostile nations and of third states.   But no matter how war is terminated, in the United States the courts generally make a practice of looking to the political departments for the date of its conclusion.

In the case of the American Civil War no declaration marked its beginning and no treaty brought it to an end. The courts of necessity were forced to the question: " When did the rebellion . . . end? " [136]   And the answer was found in two proclamations of the President: " So there were two Proclamations declaring that the war had closed; the first, issued April 2, 1866,[137] embraces the States of Virginia, North Carolina, South Carolina, Georgia, Florida, Mississippi, Tennessee, Alabama, Louisiana, and Arkansas; and the second, issued on the 20th of August, 1866,[138] embracing the State of Texas." [139]

In the case of *United States* v. *Anderson*,[140] involving the " Act to Provide for the Collection of Abandoned Property," [141] passed March 12, 1863, a provision of which served to protect the property of the Southerner loyal to the Union, by granting him the opportunity of preferring a claim against the United States for the value of his property sold by the Government, the court was faced with the problem of when the war ceased, since, according to the Act, all claims had to be submitted within two years after the end of the war. And it was clear, said the court, " that the limitation applied to the entire suppression of the rebellion, and that no one was intended to be affected by its suppression in any particu-

---

[135] For example, state succession.   See Charles G. Fenwick, *International Law*, p. 11.
[136] The *Protector*, 12 Wall. 701 (1871).
[137] 14 *Stat. L.* 811.
[138] 14 *Stat. L.* 814.
[139] *Adger* v. *Alston*, 15 Wall. 555 (1873).
[140] 9 Wall. 56 (1870).   [141] 12 *Stat. L.* 820.

lar locality." [142]   In expressing the opinion of the court, Mr. Justice Davis said:

> In a foreign war, a treaty of peace would be the evidence of the time when it closed; but in a domestic war, like the late one, some public proclamation or legislation would seem to be required to inform those whose private rights were affected by it, of the time when it terminated, and we are of the opinion that Congress did not intend that the limitation in this act should begin to run until this was done. There are various Acts of Congress and Proclamations of the President bearing on the subject, but in the view we take of this case, it is only necessary to notice the Proclamation of the President, of August 20, 1866,[143] and the Act of Congress of the 2d of March, 1867.[144]

In the former, President Johnson declared that " the said insurrection is at an end, and that peace, order, tranquility and civil authority now exist in and throughout the whole of the United States of America." [145]   By the Act of March 2,[146] Congress accepted the President's proclamation of August 20, 1866, as marking the end of the war.

However, for the purposes of the court in most of the cases following *United States* v. *Anderson,* the court found that the date of the termination of the war in the given locality was the pertinent date, rather than the date of the end of the conflict as a whole.   Accordingly, it applied the presidential proclamation which included the state where the controversy arose.   In so doing, the court sought the answer to the political question in the data produced by the political departments, at the same time recognizing by implication that the question of when the war ended should be answered, not in *vacuo,* but in relation to the purpose for which the question was asked.[147]

It would seem that the court in so construing the " Act to Provide for the Collection of Abandoned Property," was attempting to offer to " loyal " Southerners every oppor-

---

[142] 9 Wall. 69.

[143] 14 *Stat. L.* 814.   [145] 14 *Stat. L.* 817.

[144] 9 Wall. 70.   [146] *Ibid.*, 422.

[147] See *Brown* v. *Hiatts,* 15 Wall. 177 (1873) ; *Batesville Institute* v. *Kauffman,* 18 Wall. 151 (1873) ; *Ross* v. *Jones,* 22 Wall. 576 (1875) ; *Carrol* v. *Green,* 92 U. S. 509 (1876) ; *Raymond* v. *Thomas,* 91 U. S. 712 (1876) ; *Lamar* v. *Brown,* 92 U. S. 187 (1876) ; *Williams* v. *Bruffy,* 96 U. S. 176 (1877).

tunity to present claims for property confiscated and sold by the United States. In the case of *United States* v. *Anderson,* the judgment of the Court of Claims, which had decided that Anderson was entitled to recover a specific sum of money for his property, which had been originally located in South Carolina, was affirmed. The fact that the court chose the second proclamation ending the war in Texas, rather than the first which ended the war in South Carolina and other states, thus extended the effect of the statute of limitations and reflected a wise policy of reconstruction. In view of this it is at least comprehensible why the court chose the presidential proclamation of August 20, 1866, as marking the end of the war.

The Spanish-American war was brought to a close by treaty,[148] and a case arising out of the struggle, and of interest here, was *Hijo* v. *United States.*[149] This was an action brought by Hijo, a Spanish corporation, to recover the sum of $10,000 as the value of the use of a certain vessel taken by the United States army and navy in the course of the war. The complainants held that the ship was used after hostilities had ceased and peace reestablished between Spain and the United States, and it was for this period of time, August 12, 1898, the date of the protocol[150] to " some time in April, 1899, when the War Department ordered its return to the owner,"[151] that Hijo wished to recover the above mentioned sum for the use of the vessel. But, said the court, " the protocol worked a mere truce. The President had not the power to terminate the war by treaty without the advice and consent of the Senate of the United States. If a treaty be silent as to when it is to become effective, the weight of authority is that it does not become so until ratified, and this was not done until April 12, 1899[152]. . . and the war did not end by treaty until then, and all the use made by

---

[148] Treaty of Paris, December 10, 1898, *Senate Document,* no. 62, 55th Cong., 3d sess.

[149] 194 U. S. 315 (1904).

[150] Treaty of Peace with Spain, *S. Doc.,* no. 62, 55th Cong., 3d sess., p. 282.

[151] 194 U. S. 316.   [152] 30 *Stat. L.* 1754.

the government of the vessel was justified by the rules of war, without compensation." [153]

But there are other methods, in the legal sense, of bringing a war to a close. Actual hostilities in the World War came to an end with the signing of the Armistice,[154] and the Treaty of Versailles [155] terminated the struggle legally for the Allied Powers with the exception of the United States. Consequently, the courts, for three years following the Armistice, were deluged with cases which involved the date of the termination of the war, and judges were forced to the conclusion that the war between the United States and the Central Powers had not yet come to an end.[156] In one case,[157] however, raising the question as to the war powers of Congress in the suppression of disorderly houses, the judge in his opinion maintained that the war had ended, and based his decision on a statement of President Wilson before both houses of Congress. In the course of his message, the President had said: " The war thus comes to an end. . . . We know only that this tragical war, whose consuming flame swept from one nation to another until all the world was on fire, is at an end. . . ." [158] It was decided in this case, that since peace existed, the war-time power of Congress anent disorderly houses, reverted to the states. But in a later case,[159] the Armistice was declared not to have ended the war. This case raised the question of the validity of the war-time Prohibition Act [160] and its applicability at the time of the hearing, dependent of course, upon the date of

---

[153] 194 U. S. 317.

[154] November 11, 1918.   [155] June 28, 1919.

[156] *Nueces Valley Town-Site Company* v. *McAdoo*, 257 Fed. 143 (1919); *United States* v. *Russel*, 265 Fed. 414 (1920); *Weed* v. *Lockwood*, 266 Fed. 785 (1920); *United States* v. *Steene*, 263 Fed. 130 (1920); *Bentall* v. *United States*, 276 Fed. 121 (1921); *Ex parte Sichofsky*, 273 Fed. 694 (1921); *Weisman* v. *United States*, 271 Fed. 944 (1921); *Vincenti* v. *United States*, 272 Fed. 114 (1921); *United States* v. *Wallis*, 278 Fed. 838 (1921).

[157] *United States* v. *Hicks*, 256 Fed. 707 (1919).

[158] *Cong. Rec.*, 65th Cong., 2d sess., pp. 11, 538. This statement, however, was not accepted by Congress as marking the close of the war.

[159] *Hamilton* v. *Kentucky Distilleries Co.*, 251 U. S. 146 (1919).

[160] 40 *Stat. L.* 1045-1046.

the termination of the war; but as Justice Brandeis said in the opinion, " for aught that appears, it has not yet terminated." [161]   Chief Justice White, in the opinion of the case of *Kahn* v. *Anderson*,[162] said that " complete peace, in the legal sense, had not come to pass by the effect of the Armistice and the cessation of hostilities." [163]

It has generally been accepted that the proper, or legal, conclusion of a state of war in the international sense, is a treaty.[164]   Yet, on July 2, 1921, Congress by joint resolution,[165] terminated the war as far as concerned the courts; this was considered by the courts sufficient evidence that the political departments had brought the war to its legal end. For example, a demand by the Alien Property Custodian for property, signed before, but not served until after the unilateral termination of the war by Congress, was held ineffective to vest title to the property in the Custodian.[166] Thus was the joint resolution considered by the courts, in spite of the fact that the war did not end in the international sense until the treaty of peace with Germany.[167]

The recognition of the existence of a state of war has been treated, more or less incidentally, in the foregoing, but it may be said that whether the United States is involved or not, such a question is deemed a political one; that is, " the condition of peace or war, public or civil, in a legal sense must be determined by the political departments, not the judicial." [168]   Mr. Justice Story, in the case of the *Santissima Trinidad*,[169] said that " the government of the United States has recognized the existence of a civil war between Spain and her colonies, and has avowed a determination to remain neutral between the parties. . . . Each party is,

---

[161] *Hamilton* v. *Kentucky Distilleries Co.*, 251 U. S. 168.

[162] 255 U. S. 1 (1921).

[163] *Ibid.*, 9.

[164] See *United States* v. *Anderson*, 9 Wall. 56 (1870); and *Hijo* v. *United States*, 194 U. S. 315 (1904).

[165] 42 *Stat. L.* (Part 1) 105.

[166] *Miller* v. *Rouse*, 276 Fed. 715 (1921).

[167] 42 *Stat. L.* (Part 2) 1939.

[168] *United States* v. *One Hundred and Twenty-Nine Packages*, Fed. Cas. 15,941 (1862).

[169] 7 Wheat. 283 (1822).

therefore deemed by us a belligerent nation, having so far as concerns us, the sovereign rights of war, and entitled to be respected in the exercise of those rights." [170]   The rule is applicable at the present time.   In a recent case it was said that " recognition either of belligerency or independence is a political act, which must be exercised by the political branches of government, the executive and legislative." [171]

IV

To turn from the recognition of belligerency to the recognition of states, it may be said at once that the purpose is to discuss the latter, not from the point of view of international law, but of constitutional law.   Every nation may recognize a colony in revolt, let us say, of Great Britain, as an independent and sovereign state.   But let it be supposed that the United States has withheld recognition.   Were this the case, the hypothetical state, as far as concerned the United States, would still be in revolt, non-independent, non-sovereign, and legally outside the family of nations; legally and politically the state would still be a colony owing allegiance to her former sovereign.   Furthermore, until the

---

[170] *Ibid.*   See also *Neustra Senora de la Caridad,* 4 Wheat. 497 (1819).

[171] *Waldes* v. *Basch,* 179 N. Y. Supp. 713 (1919).   See also *United States* v. *Palmer,* 3 Wheat. 610 (1818) ; the *Divina Pastora,* 4 Wheat. 52 (1819) ; the *Estrella,* 4 Wheat. 298 (1819).

The belligerent or insurgent character of a revolutionary movement is also considered a political question.   In the case of *United States* v. *The Three Friends,* 166 U. S. 1 (1897), it is said that " it belongs to the political department to determine when belligerency shall be recognized, and its action must be accepted. . . .   The distinction between recognition of belligerency and recognition of a condition of political revolt, between recognition of the existence of war in a material sense and of war in a legal sense, is sharply illustrated by the case before us.   For here the political department has not recognized the existence of a *de facto* belligerent power engaged in hostility with Spain, but has recognized the existence of insurrectionary warfare. . . ."

The courts have also considered the need for, and the status of, certain acts of retaliation, political questions.   This is well illustrated in the case of the *Nereide,* 9 Cranch 388 (1815).   Here it was said that " the court is decidedly of opinion that reciprocating to the subjects of a nation, or retaliating on them its unjust proceedings towards our citizens, is a political, not a legal measure.   It is for the consideration of the government, not of its courts."

political departments of the government had by some act recognized the new state, the courts of the United States would be bound by the previous relationship. In other words, the matter of recognition is a political question.

Rose v. *Himely* [172] is a case in point. This was a claim for a cargo of coffee and other products, which, after being shipped on an American vessel, the " Sarah," from a seaport in Santo Domingo, at that time in the hands of revolutionists, was captured by a French privateer and carried into Baracoa, a port of Cuba, where it was sold by its captors. The cargo was brought by the purchaser into South Carolina where it was libelled by the original owner, a citizen of the United States. Subsequent to this action, and while lying in the waters of South Carolina, the cargo was condemned by a French court sitting in Santo Domingo.

The respondent (the purchaser of the cargo at Baracoa) maintained, first, that the condemnation of the vessel and cargo by the French court was in exercise of belligerent rights and not for violation of a municipal law; and second, that the condemnation of the vessel was valid even though, at the time the " Sarah " was lying in the waters of a neutral country. The latter claim was briefly considered by the court; in fact, the decision of restitution to the original owner rested upon the well-established principle of law that no admiralty or prize court may proceed against a vessel which is not within its jurisdiction, because it has no power over the *res.* As to the first claim, if the contention that the condemnation by the French court was a part of the exercise of belligerent rights, then France had " incontestibly by the law of nations the right of punishing that interference by the seizure and condemnation of our ships and goods found in contravention." [173] It was argued that Santo Domingo had declared itself a sovereign state, that since the colony maintained its sovereignty by arms, it must be considered and treated by other nations as sovereign in fact, entitled to maintain the same intercourse with the world maintained by other belligerent nations. But here the dic-

---

[172] 4 Cranch 241 (1808).   [173] *Ibid.*, 258 (footnote).

tum was stated by Marshall, and for our purposes this is important, that "it is for governments to decide whether they will consider St. Domingo as an independent nation, and until such decision shall be made, or France shall relinquish her claim, courts of justice must consider the ancient state of things as remaining unaltered, and the sovereign power of France over that colony as still subsisting." [174] And since the political departments of the government of the United States had not recognized the independence of Santo Domingo the courts of the United States were controlled by the previous relationship between mother-country and colony.

The 1818 term of the Supreme Court was notable "for the decision of one case and the argument of another which marked the court's importance as a factor in American history." [175] One of these cases was *Dartmouth College* v. *Woodward*,[176] familiar to all; the other was *Gelston* v. *Hoyt*,[177] which is of interest to us here. In this case the venerable principle of Anglo-Saxon law, namely, that no man, not excepting the President of the United States, is above the law, was reaffirmed.

Gelston v. *Hoyt* [178] involved the question whether or not certain government officials, who had been sued for damages as the result of the seizure of a vessel under the alleged authority of neutrality laws, could, by alleging that the act was done by express order of the President, James Madison, justify the seizure. It was alleged that the vessel in question was fitted out and equipped with the intention that she should be employed in the service of a foreign prince or state, namely, of that part of Santo Domingo under the government of Petion, against that part of the island which was governed by Christophe, another prince, and which constituted another state. The court, speaking through Justice

---

[174] *Ibid.*, 272. And as a matter of interest, it was deemed by the court "to be sufficiently evident that the seizure and confiscation are made in consequence of a violation of municipal regulation, and not in right of war."

[175] Warren, I, 474.
[176] 4 Wheat. 518 (1819).
[177] 3 Wheat. 246 (1818).
[178] *Ibid.*

Story, held that since no statute delegated authority to the President to direct seizure by civil officials, the order in effect did not protect them, particularly if the rights of individuals were violated.

But counsel for the plaintiffs-in-error maintained that a vessel allegedly fitted out by a private citizen for the above service was contrary to the Act of June 5, 1794,[179] which provided that " if any person shall within any of the ports, harbors, bays, rivers or other waters of the United States, fit out and arm or attempt to fit out and arm . . . any ship or vessel with intent that such ship or vessel shall be employed in the service of any foreign prince or state to cruise or commit hostilities upon the subjects, citizens or property of another foreign prince or state with whom the United States are at peace . . . every such person so offending shall upon conviction be adjudged guilty of a high misdemeanor. . . ." [180]   It was also maintained that Santo Domingo was independent of all connection with France and counsel called upon the court to accept the *de facto* situation in place of a formal acknowledgment of it by governments. Had the court acceded to this view, it would perhaps have upheld the seizure by the plaintiffs-in-error by virtue of the Act of June 5.

As Justice Story pointed out, no evidence was offered to the effect that either of these governments, that of Petion or that of Christophe, had been recognized by the governments of the United States or France.   " No doctrine," continued Justice Story, " is better established than that it belongs exclusively to governments to recognize new states in the revolutions which may occur in the world; and until such recognition, either by our own government, or the government to which the new state belonged,[181] courts of justice are bound to consider the ancient state of things as remaining unaltered." [182]   And to the knowledge of the court

---

[179] 1 *Stat. L.* 381.
[180] *Ibid.*, 383.
[181] This would not automatically result in recognition by the United States.
[182] 3 Wheat. 324.

" neither the government of Petion nor Christophe have ever been recognized as a foreign state, by the government of the United States, or of France." [183]

United States v. *Klintock* [184] is another case in point. Klintock, a citizen of the United States, was charged with having committed piracy on the high seas. The vessel in which he sailed was registered outside the United States, and cruised under a commission from a certain Aury, a Brigadier of the Mexican Republic and Generalissimo of the Floridas. The counsel for Klintock contended, as one of the grounds for the prisoner's release, that the commission given Klintock by Aury exempted him from the charge of piracy, but the court did not accept this view. Speaking for the court, Chief Justice Marshall said: " So far as this court can take any cognizance of that fact, Aury can have no power, either as Brigadier of the Mexican Republic, a republic of whose existence we know nothing, or as Generalissimo of the Floridas, a province in the possession of Spain, to issue commissions to authorize private or public vessels to make captures at sea." [185]

The case of *Kennett* v. *Chambers* [186] concerned a contract entered into by General T. J. Chambers of the Texan army, and Kennett and others, whereby the latter agreed to assist General Chambers in outfitting and arming a Texan army, the sole purpose of which was to gain the independence of Texas, at the time under the sovereignty of Mexico. This assistance was to be effected by the transfer of the private estate of Chambers to Kennett in return for the sum of twelve thousand, five hundred dollars, to be paid in installments. It was contended that the property had been paid for, but, that Chambers under divers pretexts had failed to convey the land according to the provisions of the agreement.

It is obvious that the validity of the contract in this case depended upon the relations of Texas, Mexico and the United

---

[183] *Ibid.*, 325.
[184] 5 Wheat. 144 (1820); see also *Consul of Spain* v. *The Conception*, 6 Wheat. 235 (1821).
[185] 5 Wheat. 149.   [186] 14 How. 38 (1852).

States. A few months previous to the date of the agreement entered into by the contestants, Texas had declared her independence. However, this independence had not been recognized by the United States; consequently, the treaties and agreements between the United States and Mexico were still in force, and such being the case, by the Constitution of the United States, were the supreme law of the land binding citizen as well as government, and " no contract could lawfully be made in violation of their provisions." [187] Thus, the question as to whether Texas was an independent state arose, for if Texas were independent, the contract would have held, and so the court turned to the political departments for a solution.

It is a sufficient answer to the argument to say that the question of whether Texas had or had not at that time become an independent state, was a question for that department of our government exclusively which is charged with out foreign relations. And until the period when that department recognized it as an independent state, the judicial tribunals of the country were bound to consider the old order of things as having continued, and to regard Texas as a part of the Mexican territory. And, if we undertook to inquire whether she had not in fact become an independent sovereign state before she was recognized as such by the treaty-making power, we should take upon ourselves the exercise of political authority, for which a judicial tribunal is wholly unfit, and which the Constitution has conferred exclusively upon another department. [188]

It may be added that the contract referred to in this case was declared illegal and void.

To turn to the matter of the recognition of governments as a political question it has been said that " in judicial proceedings involving the question of the existence of a particular government, the action of the Department of State ' has been confined to furnishing, upon application of any court, a statement of the actual status of diplomatic relations between the United States and the government in question.' " [189] And the determinations of the Department of State, a political department of the national government,

---

[187] *Ibid.*, 46.
[188] *Ibid.*, 50-51.
[189] Secretary of State, John W. Foster to Senor Bolet Peraya, Venezuelan minister to the United States, September 21, 1892. Quoted in Moore, I, 247.

are accepted by the courts without hesitance. Questions of this nature are without the province of the courts, and hence, it is to the political departments that the judiciary turns for knowledge as to the position of a foreign government in respect to the government of the United States. For example, in the case of *Jones* v. *United States*,[190] the question arose as to the right of a United States court to jurisdiction over an island in the Caribbean, Navassa Island, acquired by the United States by right of discovery and occupation. In the opinion of the court, Mr. Justice Gray said: "Who is the sovereign *de jure* or *de facto* of a territory is not a judicial, but a political, question, the determination of which by the legislative and executive departments of any government conclusively binds the judges, as well as all other officers, citizens and subjects, of that government." [191]

In 1892 a revolution occurred in Venezuela, the principal parties to which were Palacio of the faction in power, and Crespo, the anti-administration chief. General Hernandez belonged to the Crespo party and commanded its victorious forces at Buena Vista. October 6, 1892 saw the capital taken by the revolutionists, and, on the twenty-third of the month, the Crespo government was recognized as the legiti-

---

[190] 137 U. S. 202 (1890). See also the earlier case, the *Nueva Anna*, 6 Wheat. 193 (1821).

[191] *Ibid.* Henry Jones was tried and convicted for murder committed on Navassa Island, a Guano island, in a United States court of Admiralty. The counsel for the defense contended that the Guano law of August 18, 1856 (11 *Stat. L.* 119) was unconstitutional on the ground that an act or deed to come under admiralty must arise wholly upon the sea. This Act provided (sec. 6) that "until otherwise provided by law, all acts done, and offences or crimes committed, on every such island, rocks, or keys, by persons who may land thereon, or in the waters adjacent thereto, shall be held and deemed to have been done or committed on the high seas, on board a merchant ship or vessel belonging to the United States, and be punished according to the laws of the United States relating to such ships or vessels and offences on the high seas; which laws, for the purposes aforesaid, are hereby extended to and over such islands, rocks, or keys." In reply to the charge of unconstitutionality the court said: "By the Constitution . . . while a crime committed within any state must be tried in that state and in a district previously ascertained by law, yet a crime not committed within any state of the Union may be tried at such place as Congress may by law have directed." See art. 2, sec. 2 of the Constitution.

mate government by the United States. It so happened that an American citizen, G. F. Underhill, under the old régime in Venezuela, had constructed a water system for the city of Bolivar. After the entry of General Hernandez into the city, Underhill applied for a passport in order to leave the country. This Hernandez refused to issue at the time, but shortly afterwards, and previous to the recognition of the Crespo government by the United States,[192] a passport was issued to Underhill, who immediately left the country. Out of this detention caused by reason of the refusal of Hernandez to issue a passport, and bolstered by alleged assaults and affronts, arose the case of *Underhill* v. *Hernandez*.[193]

This case was heard first in the Circuit Court of the United States for the Eastern District of New York and then in the United States Circuit Court of Appeals for the Second Circuit, and in both instances the verdict was against the plaintiff, Underhill. The suit was then carried to the Supreme Court on certiorari. " In this case," said Chief Justice Fuller, " the archives of the state department show that civil war was flagrant in Venezuela from the spring of 1892; that the revolution was successful; and that the revolutionary government was recognized by the United States as the government of the country, it being, to use the language of the Secretary of State in a communication to our minister to Venezuela, ' accepted by the people, in the possession of the power of the nation and fully established.' " [194] " That these were facts of which the court is bound to take judicial notice, and for information as to which it may consult the Department of State, there can be no doubt." [195] And it was decided, therefore, by the court, that to consider the actions and proceedings of the triumphant Crespo party as acts of banditti or mobs was " idle." [196] Underhill's complaints against Hernandez were dismissed since the acts of the latter were the " acts of a military commander representing

---

[192] Underhill was given the passport on October 18, 1892; United States recognized the Crespo Government, October 23, 1892.
[193] 168 U. S. 250 (1897).
[194] *Ibid.*, 253.   [195] *Ibid.*   [196] *Ibid.*

the authority of the revolutionary party as a government, which afterwards [197] succeeded and was recognized by the United States." [198]

Another case arising out of the Latin-American imbroglio was that of *Oetjen* v. *The Central Leather Company*,[199] a suit in replevin, involving the title to a consignment of hides. It is necessary, in order to understand the case, to discuss its background.

February 23, 1913, brought the assassination of Madero, the President of the Mexican Republic. Shortly thereafter, General Huerta declared himself provisional president and took oath of office as such. On March 26 of the same year, Carranza, then governor of Coahuila, initiated a revolution against the authority of Huerta and proclaimed the organization of a constitutional régime. Now, when Carranza assumed leadership of the Constitutional forces, he commissioned Fransisco Villa his representative and assigned him to an independent command in northern Mexico. By the fall of the year, the Constitutionalist faction was in possession of fully two-thirds of the country.

Villa captured the town of Torreon, in the state of Coahuila, on October first, and immediately demanded that the inhabitants contribute a certain sum of money for the support of his troops. But one Martinez, a wealthy resident of the town and a dealer in hides, on the advance of Villa's army, had fled, and thus failed to pay the assessment. In lieu of cash, Villa confiscated the hides of the vanished Martinez and sold them to a Texas corporation, Finnegan-Brown Company. The hides, paid for in Mexico, were shipped into the United States and there replevied. The plaintiff-in-error

---

[197] *Ibid.* "If the party seeking to dislodge the existing government succeeds, and the independence of the government it has set up is recognized, then the acts of such government from the commencement of its existence are regarded as those of an independent nation." Recognition is retroactive and dates back to the time of the acquisition of power by the newly recognized state. The effect of recognition is to render ineffectual any attempt on the part of the courts of the recognizing state to declare legislative and executive acts, past and future of the recently established government, illegal.

[198] *Ibid.*, 254.

[199] 246 U. S. 297 (1918).

(Oetjen) claimed to own the hides as an assignee of Martinez and Company, while the defendant-in-error made the same claim on the ground of purchase from the Texas corporation alleged to have bought the hides in Mexico from Villa. In the lower court,[200] judgment was rendered for the defendant-in-error; subsequently, the case was carried to the Supreme Court, it being contended that "the claim of title to the hides by the defendant-in-error is invalid because based upon a purchase from General Villa, who, it is urged, confiscated them contrary to the provisions of the Hague Convention of 1907 [201] respecting the laws and customs of war on land." [202]

The court first took judicial notice of the fact that since the events outlined above and since the appearance of the controversy in the court of first instance, the Carranza government had been recognized by the United States, first as the *de facto*,[203] and later as the *de jure* [204] government of the Republic of Mexico.

With the contention that the Hague Convention had been violated, the court dealt briefly, stating that the Hague Conventions were international in character, that they were intended to regulate international warfare and not civil war.

It was the pleasure of the court to base its decision on three established principles of law, the first of which was that "the conduct of the foreign relations of our government is committed by the Constitution to the executive and legislative—'the political'—departments of the Government, and the propriety of what may be done in the exercise of this political power is not subject to judicial inquiry or decision." [205] Continuing, the court quoted *Jones* v. *United States* [206] to the effect that the determination of the *de facto* or *de jure* sovereign of a particular territory is not a judicial but a political question. The second principle concerned

---

[200] 87 N. J. Law, 552, 94 Atl. 789.
[201] See *Proceedings of the Hague Peace Conference, Conference of 1907*, I, 623.
[202] 246 U. S. 299.
[203] October 19, 1915.
[204] August 31, 1917.
[205] 246 U. S. 302.
[206] 137 U. S. 202 (1890).

the retroactive force of recognition; and the third, the respect due the independence of every other sovereign state, in particular that the "courts of one country will not sit in judgment on the acts of the government of another done within its own territory." [207]

The court applied these principles of law to the case, stating that "we have a duly commissioned military commander of what must be accepted as the legitimate government of Mexico, in the progress of a revolution, and when conducting active independent operations, seizing and selling in Mexico, as a military contribution, the property in controversy, at the time owned and in possession of a citizen of Mexico, the assignor of the plaintiff-in-error. Plainly this was the action, in Mexico, of the legitimate Mexican government when dealing with a Mexican citizen, and, as we have seen, for the soundest reasons, and upon repeated decisions of this court such action is not subject to re-examination and modification by the courts of this country." [208] Thus, in summary, it is seen that in its decision, involving as it did the recognition of the Carranza government, the court did not weigh the facts and events to conclude that the government in question was the *de facto* or *de jure* government of Mexico; in fact, the court contended that this was outside of its legitimate sphere and within the sphere of the executive and legislative departments.

This was true also of a recent case in which the plaintiff, The Russian Socialist Federated Soviet Government, was not permitted to bring suit in a court of the United States.[209] The case was decided in a lower court, but, since the decision rested mainly upon various decisions of the Supreme Court, its consideration will not be.out of place in this study. The facts of the case need not be stated. "In the case at bar," said Judge Dowling, "while plaintiff claims to be a *de facto* government, and its title and right to sue alike rest

---

[207] Here the court quoted *Underhill* v. *Hernandez*, 168 U. S. 250 (1897).

[208] 246 U. S. 303.

[209] *Russian Socialist Federated Soviet Government* v. *Cibrario*, 191 N. Y. Supp. 543 (1921).

on that claim, it is unable to show any acts of recognition by the government of this country. On the contrary, the record proves that, so far as this country is concerned, the plaintiff is non-existent as a sovereignty." [210]   In other words, there had been no action on the part of the political departments of the United States giving notice of recognition of the Soviet government. In conclusion, Judge Dowling said: " All these facts appearing without contradiction, it follows that plaintiff, never having been recognized as a sovereignty by the executive or legislative branches of the United States government, has no capacity to sue in the courts of this country." [211]

However, in *Salimoff* v. *Standard Oil Company*,[212] the New York Court of Appeals, accepting the position of the Department of State, recognized the Soviet government as the *de facto* government of Russia. The government of Russia, by a nationalization decree, confiscated all oil lands in Russia, extracted oil, and sold it to the Standard Oil Company. The former owners, Russian nationals, joined " in equitable action for an accounting on the ground that the confiscatory decrees of the unrecognized Soviet government and the seizure of oil lands thereunder have no other effect in law on the rights of parties than seizure by bandits. . . ." [213]   The court was thus presented with the question of the effect " on the title of a purchaser from the unrecognized confiscating Soviet Russian government." [214]

The court turned to the Department of State, a political department, for some indication as to the status of the Soviet government. In a memorandum submitted to the court by the Department of State it was said that " the

[210] *Ibid.*, 549-550.

[211] *Ibid.*, 550. See also *Russian Reinsurance Company* v. *Stoddard*, 240 N. Y. 149 (1925) and *Petrogradsky Mejdunarodny Kommerchesky Bank* v. *The National City Bank*, 253 N. Y. 23 (1930). In this connection see Edwin M. Borchard, " The Unrecognized Government in American Courts," *American Journal of International Law*, XXVI, 261; Louis Connick, " The Effect of Soviet Decrees in American Courts," *Yale Law Journal*, XXXIV, 499; and Louis L. Jaffe, *Judicial Aspects of Foreign Relations*.

[212] 262 N. Y. 220 (1933).

[213] *Ibid.*, 223.   [214] *Ibid.*

Department of State is cognizant of the fact that the Soviet régime is exercising control and power in territory of the former Russian Empire and the Department of State has no disposition to ignore that fact." [215]   The memorandum also stated that " the refusal of the Government of the United States to accord recognition to the Soviet régime is not based on the ground that that régime does not exercise control and authority in territory of the former Russian Empire, but on other facts." [216]   In line with this memorandum of the State Department, Chief Justice Pound declared that " the courts may not recognize the Soviet government as the *de jure* government until the State Department gives the word. They may, however, say that it is a government maintaining peace and order, providing for national defense and the general welfare, carrying on relations with our own government and others." [217]   The conclusion of the court was that the Soviet government could not be ignored " so far as the validity of its acts in Russia is concerned." [218]   It was held, therefore, that since the Soviet government committed no wrong under its laws,[219] the plaintiffs had not stated a cause of action.

A manifestation of recognition of one government by another is the exchange of diplomatic representatives. The ambassador, or chargé d'affaires, arriving on the shores of the receiving state has a peculiar status. He is not a citizen, yet he enjoys greater legal freedom than does a citizen. No one can, with impunity, offend him. He is enveloped in a cloud of inviolability; he is not subject to prosecution, and free to conduct himself as he will in the discharge of his duties. He may contract debts and fail to pay them; he may malign the reputation of a citizen, yet the courts cannot entertain suit against him. The accrediting state can only be requested to recall him.

However, there have been suits brought into the courts in which, in one way or another, diplomatic representatives were

---

[215] *Ibid.*, 224.   [217] *Ibid.*, 227.
[216] *Ibid.*   [218] *Ibid.*, 228.
[219] "According to the law of nations it did no legal wrong when it confiscated the oil of its own nationals and sold it in Russia to the defendants." *Ibid.*, 227.

involved. Such ministers naturally claim diplomatic immunity. But the court does not itself investigate the status of a person claiming such immunity; instead, it is to the Department of State that the court turns for such information and the word of this political department is final. To state that the status of a diplomatic representative is a political question is to state what is already obvious.

Mr. Justice Washington in the case of *United States* v. *Ortega* said: " The constitution of the United States having vested in the president the power to receive ambassadors and other public ministers, has necessarily bestowed upon that branch of the government, not only the right, but the exclusive right, to judge of the credentials of the ministers so received; and so long as they continue to be recognized and treated by the president as ministers, the other branches of the government are bound to consider them as such. If the courts of justice could sit in judgment upon the decision of the executive in reference to the public character of a foreign minister, and pronouncing him to be unduly appointed, or improperly recognized, deprive him of the privileges of a minister, what an extraordinary anomaly would such an interference present to the world." [220]

The case of *Ex parte Hitz* [221] involved the application of one Hitz for a writ of certiorari commanding the Supreme Court of the District of Columbia to certify to the Supreme Court of the United States the indictment and subsequent proceedings against him in the District Court, on the ground that, when the indictment was filed, he was a duly accredited diplomatic representative of the Swiss Confederation, recognized by the Department of State. Applying to the State Department, the court learned that, at the time of the indictment, Hitz was not recognized as a diplomatic representative, and the application was denied.[222]

---

[220] Fed. Cas. 15,971 (1825).
[221] 111 U. S. 766 (1884).
[222] See also *Ex parte Baiz*, 135 U. S. 403 (1890).

CHAPTER III

CLASSIFICATION AND ANALYSIS OF SOME CASES INVOLVING "POLITICAL QUESTIONS" CONCLUDED

I

In the foregoing discussion our attention has been directed only incidentally toward the matter of treaties. We find, however, involved in the general problem of international agreements, certain questions of interest which may be denominated political. These are questions arising out of the negotiation of treaties, their violation, termination or continued validity, and interpretation. The Constitution declares that "the judicial power shall extend to all cases, in law and equity, arising under this Constitution, the laws of the United States, and treaties made, or which shall be made," [1] under the authority of the United States; but the judicial power in practice extends, as far as treaties are concerned, only to those which "confer private rights on citizens or subjects of the contracting powers—rights such as are enforceable in a court of justice," [2] and in such cases "the courts accept such treaties as rules of decision and place upon them their own interpretation. . . ." [3] But, exclusive of private rights, the questions as to whether a treaty has been violated or terminated, or whether the interpretation by the executive or legislative departments is correct, or whether a treaty has been properly negotiated, are not for the courts but for the political departments to decide.

Doe v. *Braden*,[4] a controversy arising out of the treaty with Spain [5] by which the Floridas were ceded to the United States, is a case in point. On January 24, 1818, on the strength of a proposal of the Spanish government to cede the Floridas to the United States, negotiations between the

---

[1] Art. 1, sec. 2.
[2] John M. Mathews, *Conduct of American Foreign Relations*, p. 219.
[3] *Ibid.*
[4] 16 How. 635 (1853).   [5] 8 *Stat. L.* 252.

two governments were begun in Washington. Over a year later a treaty was signed,[6] the terms of which necessitated an exchange of ratifications within six months. But, after the King of Spain had authorized his ministers to negotiate the treaty, and after negotiations had actually begun, the King made three grants of territory, located in the Floridas, to three of his subjects. These were not insignificant grants, but "covered all or nearly all of the public domain in the territory proposed to be ceded."[7] As a result the United States made an addition to the treaty to the effect that "all grants made since the 24th of January, 1818" were "declared and agreed to be null and void."[8] Grants made prior to that date were confirmed. And with this added provision, the treaty was ratified[9] by the President of the United States by and with the advice and consent of the Senate.

However, another difficulty arose. Before the ratifications had been exchanged, Mr. Adams, then Secretary of State, was informed that the Duke of Alagon, a subject of the King of Spain and a beneficiary of one of the above-mentioned grants, intended to rely upon a royal order of December 17, 1817, as sufficient to convey to him the land from that date; and, furthermore, he claimed that the treaty confirmed rather than annulled his title. This contention of the Duke of Alagon was vitiated by a written declaration annexed to the treaty the effect of which was to annul specifically all three grants.[10] The ratifications of this treaty and annex were exchanged on February 22, 1821, and on that day Florida became a part of the territory of the United States.

The case of *Doe* v. *Braden*[11] was an action of ejectment. The suit was brought by the plaintiff-in-error in order to recover certain lands in Florida, and the sole foundation of his title to the land was the grant from the King of Spain to the Duke of Alagon.

---

[6] February 22, 1819.   [8] 8 *Stat. L.* 258.
[7] *Doe* v. *Braden*, 16 How. 654.   [9] February 24, 1819.
[10] 16 How. 655. The three grants "were understood . . . to have been annulled by the 8th article of the Treaty." See 8 *Stat. L.* 268 ff.
[11] 16 How. 653.

The plaintiff contended that the King of Spain, by the terms of the constitution under which the Spanish government was administered, had no power to annul the grant to Alagon by treaty or in any other way; and that the Cortes was the only body in the Spanish government constitutionally privileged to do so. And, claimed the plaintiff, " it does not appear, in the ratification, that it was annulled by that body or by its authority or consent." [12]   To the arguments of the plaintiff, Chief Justice Taney declared that this was a political question belonging exclusively to the political departments, and that it was not incumbent upon the courts to annul or disregard any treaty unless it violated the provisions of the Constitution of the United States.[13] " It would be impossible," said Taney, " for the Executive Department of the government to conduct our foreign relations with any advantage to the country, and fulfill the duties which the Constitution has imposed upon it, if every court in the country was authorized to inquire and decide whether the person who ratified the treaty on behalf of a foreign nation had the power, by its Constitution and laws, to make the engagements into which he entered. . . . It was for the President and Senate to determine whether the King, by the Constitution and laws of Spain, was authorized to make this stipulation [that the grant to Alagon was annulled] and to ratify a treaty containing it. They have recognized his power by accepting this stipulation as a part of the compact, and ratifying the treaty which contains it." [14]

The plaintiff's claim that the King of Spain had no power to annul the grant of territory to Alagon, by treaty or otherwise, was held by the court to be insupportable unless the proposition could be maintained " that a court of justice may inquire whether the President and Senate were not mistaken as to the authority of the Spanish monarch in this respect; or knowingly sanctioned an act of injustice committed by him upon an individual in violation of the laws of Spain.

[12] *Ibid.*, 657.
[13] No treaty has been declared unconstitutional.
[14] 16 How. 657-658.

But it is evident that such a proposition can find no support in the Constitution of the United States; nor in the jurisprudence of any country where the judicial and political powers are separated and placed in different hands. Certainly no judicial tribunal in the United States ever claimed it, or supposed it possessed it." [15]

It is evident, on consideration of the foregoing, that the Supreme Court and other federal courts, avoided the question as to the constitutional powers and qualifications of the representatives of foreign sovereigns with whom the United States negotiates treaties. There were two reasons given by Taney for this attitude of the court. The first is that in accordance with the doctrine of the separation of powers, such questions would not properly fall within the sphere of the judiciary; and the second is expediency. The impossibility of the executive department to conduct our foreign relations expeditiously, and with united front, if every court in the country could pass upon the qualifications of the persons who ratified a treaty on behalf of a foreign country, is apparent.

The same doctrine applies to treaties entered into with Indian tribes. In the case of *Fellows* v. *Blacksmith*,[16] Mr. Justice Nelson said: " An objection was taken, on the argument, to the validity of the Treaty, on the ground that the Tonawanda band of the Seneca Indians were not represented by the chiefs and head men of the band in the negotiations and execution of it. But the answer to this is, that the Treaty, after executed and ratified by the proper authorities of the government, becomes the supreme law of the land, and the courts can no more go behind it for the purpose of annulling its effect and operation, than they can behind an Act of Congress." [17]

It has been held, also, that whether or not the provisions of a treaty have been violated by one of the contracting parties is a political question and, therefore, beyond the competence of the courts. In this respect, the early case of

---

[15] *Ibid.*, 658.
[16] 19 How. 366 (1857).   [17] *Ibid.*, 372.

Ware v. *Hylton* [18] is pertinent. This was an action for debt, brought by a British creditor against a citizen of the United States, to recover upon a bond executed before the War of Independence. This debt during the war was paid into the loan office of Virginia in pursuance of a law of that state providing for the sequestration of British property, such payment supposedly absolving the debt. Of course, the Virginia legislature was within its rights and authority in passing such a law.[19] This action would have prevented subsequent action against the debtor. However, the creditor's right to action was revived by the treaty of peace ending the war. The Treaty of Paris [20] provided that " creditors on either side shall meet with no lawful impediment to the recovery of the full value in sterling money, of all bona fide debts heretofore contracted." [21] This provision, after the adoption of the Constitution, nullified the statute passed by the Virginia assembly, destroyed the payment made under it, and revived the debt, giving the right of recovery to the creditor against the debtor.

Thus the question arose, a question of supreme significance to the relationship between the states and the Federal government, whether state laws authorizing the sequestration of British debts and payment of the same in a depreciated currency, should stand as valid against the provisions of the Treaty of Paris. It is of interest to note that in this case John Marshall appeared as counsel for the debtors. Here the man, who later was to play so eminent a rôle in the defense and development of the supremacy of the national government, supported a theory of government which was not only anathema to him, but against his own interests.[22] In his argument before the court concerning the supremacy of the treaty over state laws, he referred to " those who wish

---

[18] 3 Dall. 199 (1796).

[19] From July 4, 1776, and before the establishment of the Union, the thirteen states possessed and exercised all the rights of independent states.

[20] September 3, 1783. *Treaties and Conventions*, p. 375.

[21] *Ibid.*, p. 377.

[22] See Albert J. Beveridge, *Life of John Marshall*, II, 203 ff.

to impair the sovereignty of Virginia." [23]   However, Marshall's arguments did not prevail; the court decided that the British creditors were entitled to recover, and so settled one of the most fundamental doctrines of American law, namely, that in so far as a treaty is compatible with the Constitution, it supercedes all state legislation contrary to its terms.

In the course of the proceedings, the defendants-in-error alleged [24] that due to a certain non-compliance on the part of Great Britain with the treaty provisions, British creditors could not recover a benefit under the same treaty.   But this plea [25] was held to be untenable.   In his opinion Justice Iredell held that the plea was defective so far as concerns the violation of a treaty because " by the law of nations we have no authority upon any information or concessions of any individuals, to consider or declare it broken . . . but our judgment must be grounded on the solemn declaration of Congress alone, (to whom, I conceive, the authority is entrusted)." [26]   Here it was contended by the defendants-in-error that should Congress declare a treaty broken or violated by another power, that body would be acting in a judicial capacity, and therefore illegally.   " Surely such a thing," said Justice Iredell, " was never in the contemplation of the constitution.   If it was, a method is still wanting by which it could be executed; for, if we are to declare, whether *Great Britain* or the *United States,* have violated a treaty we ought to have some way of bringing both parties before us." [27]   Justice Iredell then described the relationship that exists between the judicial and political departments with respect to the question of treaty violation.   " It is a part of the law of nations," he said, " that if a treaty be violated by one party, it is at the option of the other party, if innocent, to declare, in consequence of the breach, that the treaty is void.   If Congress, therefore, (who, I conceive, alone have such authority under our Government) shall make such a declaration, in any case like the present,

---

[23] 3 Dall. 210.
[24] *Ibid.*, 202.
[25] *Ibid.*

[26] *Ibid.*, 260.
[27] *Ibid.*, 261.

I shall deem it my duty to regard the treaty as void, and then to forbear any share in executing it as a judge. But the same law of nations tells me, that until that declaration be made, I must regard it (in the language of the law) *valid and obligatory.*" [28]

A later case, perhaps more revealing as to why the violation of a treaty is to be determined by the political departments rather than the judiciary, is *Taylor* v. *Morton*,[29] a case involving a commercial treaty between the United States and Russia.[30] It is not necessary to discuss the case except to quote one passage from the opinion:

> Is it a judicial question, whether a treaty with a foreign sovereign has been violated by him; whether the consideration of a particular stipulation in a treaty, has been voluntarily withdrawn by one party, so that it is no longer obligatory on the other; whether the views and acts of a foreign sovereign, manifested through his representative have given just occasion to the political departments of our government to withhold the execution of a promise contained in a treaty, or to act in direct contravention of such promise? I apprehend not. These powers have not been confided by the people to the judiciary, *which has no suitable means to exercise them;* [31] but to the executive and legislative departments of our governments. They belong to diplomacy and legislation, and not to the administration of existing laws.[32]

The Constitution gives the President, by and with the advice and consent of the Senate, the power to make treaties,[33] and from this power, the right to declare a treaty violated may be implied. This does not of necessity exclude judicial determination of treaty violations for it might well be argued that under the constitutional provision that the judicial power shall extend to all cases arising under the Constitution, laws, and treaties,[34] the courts might have assumed this power. But certain practical factors have guided the courts in their willingness to leave such a question to the determination of the political departments. First of all, treaties to which the United States is a party, besides being a part

---

[28] *Ibid.*
[29] Fed. Cas. 13,799 (1855); affirmed, 2 Black 481.
[30] Treaty of Commerce and Navigation, December 18, 1832. See *Treaties and Conventions*, p. 933.
[31] Italics my own.
[32] Fed. Cas. 13,799.
[33] Art. 2, sec. 2.
[34] Art. 3, sec. 2.

of the supreme law of the land, are compacts between sovereign states, and concerned as these compacts are with matters outside judicial cognizance, that is, for example, matters of policy, the judiciary does not possess " suitable means to exercise " power with regard to their violation.   Such questions belong to those departments whose sphere of competence includes the control of international relations.   And secondly, if it were incumbent upon the courts to determine treaty violations, only chaos as far as concerned treaties, would result.   Every provision of a treaty might be subjected in the courts to an examination to determine whether or not articles 2 or 3 or 6 had been violated by one or the other of the contracting parties.   It is obvious that such a situation would lead to endless difficulties.   Irrespective of the doctrine of the separation of powers, to place the question as to whether or not a treaty has been violated in the category of political questions, is to do the expedient, and leave the determination of such problems to the political departments, for use by the courts.   At least, there is a certain singleness of action, a unanimity in the expression of attitude, which would be lacking if the question were submitted to the justices of the federal courts.

It has been contended at the bar of the Supreme Court that an act of Congress, the terms of which contravene the provisions of a treaty, constitutes a violation of the treaty. In the case of the *Cherokee Tobacco*,[35] the chief question upon which the decision depended, was the effect to be given respectively to the 107th section of the Act of 1868, and the 10th article of the treaty of 1866 between the United States and the Cherokee Nation.   The former provided that " the internal revenue laws imposing taxes on distilled spirits, fermented liquors, tobacco, snuff and cigars, shall be construed to extend to such articles produced anywhere within the exterior boundaries of the United States, whether the same shall be within a collection district or not ";[36] while the latter declared that " every Cherokee Indian and freed per-

---

[35] 11 Wall. 616 (1871).   [36] 15 *Stat. L.* 167.

son residing in the Cherokee Nation shall have the right to sell any products of his farm, including his or her live stock, or any merchandise or manufactured products, and to ship and drive the same to market without restraint, paying any tax thereon which is now or may be levied by the United States on the quantity sold outside of the Indian territory." [37] It was contended by the claimants that the 107th section of the Act was not intended to, and, furthermore, did not, apply to the Cherokee country, and that the privileges and immunities secured by the treaty were still in force. In reply, the United States maintained that to the extent of the provisions of section 107 of the Act, the treaty was annulled.

Mr. Justice Swayne, delivering the opinion of the court, said: "Treaties with Indian nations within the jurisdiction of the United States . . . cannot be more obligatory" than treaties with foreign nations; and "they have no higher sanctity; and no greater inviolability nor immunity from legislative invasion can be claimed for them. The consequences in all such cases give rise to questions which must be met by the Political Department of the Government. They are beyond the sphere of judicial cognizance. In the case under consideration the Act of Congress must prevail as if the Treaty were not an element to be considered. If a wrong has been done, the power of redress is with Congress, not with the judiciary." [38]

The Constitution declares that "this Constitution, and the Laws of the United States which shall be made in pursuance thereof; and all treaties made, or which shall be made, under the Authority of the United States, shall be the supreme law of the land; and the judges in every State shall be bound thereby. . . ." [39] Legally, neither act of Congress nor treaty has greater validity one over the other. Both are declared to be the supreme law of the land, and judges must recognize both as such. However, where there is a conflict between an act of Congress and a treaty, since both comprise the supreme law, the one last in point of time must control.

[37] 14 *Stat. L.* 799, 801.   [38] 11 Wall. 621.   [39] Art. 6, cl. 2.

Therefore, an act of Congress may supercede a prior treaty, and a treaty may supercede a prior act of Congress. This being the case, it is obvious that it is not within the power of the courts to intervene where alleged injury or wrong has been done in contravention of treaty rights by an act of Congress which supercedes it. If redress is sought, the injured party can only appeal to the political departments.

On August 3, 1882, Congress passed an act to regulate immigration [40] which provided that owners of vessels bringing passengers from foreign ports into ports of the United States should pay a duty of fifty cents for each passenger not a citizen of the United States. In the Head Money Cases,[41] the validity of this act was questioned, one of the grounds being that provisions of certain treaties with friendly powers were violated. But " so far," said Justice Miller, expressing the opinion of the court, " as the provisions in that Act may be found to be in conflict with any treaty with a foreign Nation they must prevail in all the judicial courts of this country." [42] A treaty depends for the enforcement of its provisions upon the interest of the parties to it and their willingness to cooperate. If these fail, the injured party may seek redress through diplomatic channels, or in the end resort to war; but with all this, the courts of the United States have nothing to do. In the Chinese Exclusion Case [43] it was contended that the first Chinese exclusion act [44] was in direct contravention to the provisions of the treaty of 1868,[45] and that because of the treaty, the act was invalidated. But this the court could not subscribe to: " the question whether our Government is justified in disregarding its engagements with another nation is not one for the determination of the courts." [46]

By the treaty of peace of Guadalupe Hidalgo,[47] which

---

[40] 22 *Stat. L.* 214.
[41] *Edye* v. *Robertson*, 112 U. S. 580 (1884).
[42] *Ibid.*
[43] 130 U. S. 581 (1889).
[44] 25 *Stat. L.* (50th Cong., 1st sess.) ch. 1064.
[45] *Treaties and Conventions*, p. 179.
[46] See *Whitney* v. *Robertson*, 124 U. S. 190 (1888).
[47] February 2, 1848. 9 *Stat. L.* 922.

brought to a close the only war, in the legal sense, between
the United States and Mexico, the latter ceded to the United
States a large territory, included in which is the present
state of California. By the terms of the treaty, provision
was made for the protection of private property owned by
Mexicans within this territory at the time the treaty was
negotiated. However, soon after the American occupation of
the territory, gold was discovered, and the inevitable gold
rush followed. Ranchmen, settlers, miners, holders of Mexican grants, claimed title to various lands; so that when
California was admitted into the Union, it was deemed necessary to determine the validity of private claims within the
state. For this purpose "An Act to Ascertain and Settle
the Private Land Claims in the State of California" was
passed by Congress on March 3, 1851.[48]

A case coming before the Supreme Court and involving
both treaty and act of Congress was that of *Botiller* v. *Dominguez*.[49] This was an action for ejectment. Dominguez
brought the action against Botiller in order to recover a certain tract of land in California, and based his title to the
tract on a grant made by the government of Mexico in 1834;
and even though no claim under this grant had ever been
made before the Board of Land Commissioners established
by the above-mentioned act of Congress, the lower court
decided in favor of Dominguez. Before the Supreme Court,
the counsel for the defendant-in-error maintained that the
statute was invalid since it conflicted with the provisions of
the treaty of Guadalupe Hidalgo, in so far as it violated the

---

[48] 9 *Stat. L.* 631, sec. 1. "That for the purpose of ascertaining and
settling private land claims in the State of California, a commission
shall be, and is hereby, constituted which shall consist of three commissioners," etc.

Sec. 8. "That each and every person claiming lands in California
by virtue of any right or title derived from the Spanish or Mexican
Government shall present the same to the said commissioners," etc.

Sec. 11. "That the commissioners herein provided for, and the
district and supreme courts, in deciding on the validity of any claim
brought before them under the provisions of this Act, shall be governed by the Treaty of Guadalupe Hidalgo, the law of nations, the
laws, usages, and customs of the government from which the claim
is derived," etc.

[49] 130 U. S. 238 (1889).

protection, guaranteed by the treaty, to the property of Mexican citizens. But the Supreme Court reversed the decision of the lower court. "It may be said," Justice Miller declared, "that so far as the Act of Congress is in conflict with the Treaty with Mexico, that is a matter in which the court is bound to follow the statutory enactments of its own government. If the treaty was violated by this general statute enacted for the purpose of ascertaining the validity of claims derived from the Mexican Government, it was a matter of international concern, which the two States must determine by treaty, or by such other means as enables one State to enforce upon another the obligations of a treaty. This court, in a class of cases [50] like the present, has no power to set itself up as the instrumentality for enforcing the provisions of a treaty with a foreign nation which the Government of the United States chooses to disregard." [51] Thus it is clear that the protection of private rights in territory acquired by one nation from another by treaty has been held to be an exclusive function of Congress. As Mr. Justice White said in the case of *United States* v. *Santa Fe*,[52] "the duty of protecting imperfect rights of property under treaties such as those by which territory was ceded by Mexico to the United States in 1848 and 1853, in existence at the time of such cessions, rests upon the political and not the judicial department of the government." [53]

The termination of a treaty may be accomplished by the mutual consent of the nations concerned. From the point of view of international law a treaty, "although it has neither expired, nor been dissolved, may nevertheless lose its binding force by becoming void. And such voidance may

---

[50] *The Cherokee Tobacco*, 11 Wall. 616 (1871) ; *Taylor* v. *Morton*, Fed. Cas. 13,799 (1855) ; *Head Money Cases*, 112 U. S. 580 (1884) ; *Whitney* v. *Robertson*, 124 U. S. 190 (1888).

[51] 130 U. S. 247.

[52] 165 U. S. 675 (1897). See also *United States* v. *Sandoval*, 231 U. S. 28 (1913). "The mode in which private rights of property may be secured, and the obligations imposed upon the United States by treaties fulfilled, belongs to the political departments of the government to provide."

[53] 165 U. S. 714.

have different grounds—namely, extinction of one of the two contracting parties, impossibility of execution, realization of the purpose of the treaty otherwise than by fulfillment, and lastly, extinction of such object as was concerned in a treaty." [54] Furthermore, a treaty "may lose its binding force by cancellation. The causes of cancellation are four—namely, inconsistency with International Law created subsequently to the conclusion of the treaty, violation by one of the contracting parties, subsequent change of status of one of them, and war." [55] But as far as concerns the termination of treaties, the courts know no international law; and it is not within their province to enter into the question. A treaty may have lost its effect by becoming void, or by cancellation, but, until the political departments have decided a certain treaty to be no longer effective and therefore terminated, the courts have held such treaty to be in force. In other words, it has been held by the courts that they will follow the decisions of the political departments of the government as to whether or not a treaty has been terminated.

The courts have been faced with the question, for example, as to whether a treaty was automatically terminated as a consequence of the fact that a state, with whom the United States had negotiated a treaty was incorporated within another state. *Terlinden* v. *Ames* [56] is a case in point. The essential facts of the case are as follows: the German consul at Chicago filed complaint before a commissioner of the United States, one of whose duties it is to issue warrants for the apprehension of fugitives from the law of foreign states, charging that a certain Gerhard Terlinden, subject of the King of Prussia, had committed the crimes of forgery and counterfeiting in Prussia, and had subsequently fled to the United States. The warrant was issued, placed in the hands of Ames, a United States marshal, who later apprehended Terlinden. But before any evidence had been presented to the

---

[54] L. Oppenheim, *International Law*, I, 753.
[55] *Ibid.*, pp. 754-755.
[56] 184 U. S. 270 (1902). See also the earlier case of *Mahoney* v. *United States*, 10 Wall. 62 (1870).

commissioner, Terlinden petitioned the district court for a writ of habeas corpus upon certain grounds, two of which may well be quoted:

1. No treaty or convention for the extradition of fugitives from justice exists between the United States and the German Empire,[57] and 2. that the treaty or convention for the extradition of fugitives from justice concluded between the United States and the Kingdom of Prussia on the 16th day of June, 1852, and ratified May 30, A. D. 1853, was terminated by the creation of the German Empire and the adoption of the Constitution of said Empire in A. D. 1871, and that no treaty or convention for the extradition of fugitives from justice has been concluded between the United States, on the one part, and the Kingdom of Prussia or the German Empire, on the other, since said time.[58]

J. C. Bancroft Davis, in the notes appended to a volume entitled *Treaties and Conventions Concluded between the United States and Other Powers*,[59] says:

The establishment of the German Empire in 1871, and the complex relations of its component parts to each other and to the Empire, necessarily give rise to questions as to the treaties entered into with the North German Confederation and with many of the states composing the Empire. It can not be said that any fixed rules have been established. Where a state has lost its separate existence, as in the case of Hanover and Nassau, no question can arise. Where no new treaty has been negotiated with the Empire, the treaties with the various states which have preserved a separate existence have been resorted to. The question of the existence of the extradition treaty with Bavaria was presented to the United States district court, on the application of a person accused of a forgery committed in Bavaria, to be discharged on *habeas corpus*, who was in custody after the issue of the mandate, at the request of the minister of Germany. The court held that the treaty was admitted by both Governments to be in existence.[60] Such a question is, after all, purely a political one.[61]

And so it was deemed by the court in *Terlinden* v. *Ames*. In expressing the opinion of the court, Chief Justice Fuller said: " without considering whether extinguished treaties can be renewed by tacit consent under our Constitution, we think that on the question, whether this treaty has ever been terminated, governmental action in respect to it must be

---

[57] From statement by Chief Justice Fuller, 194 U. S. 273.
[58] *Ibid.*
[59] Washington, Government Printing Office (1889).
[60] *In re Thomas*, Fed Cas. 13,887 (1874).
[61] *Treaties and Conventions*, p. 1234.

regarded as of controlling importance." [62]   And, continued Fuller, "during the period from 1871 to the present day, extradition from this country to Germany, and from Germany to this country, has been frequently granted under the treaty,[63] which has thus been repeatedly recognized by both governments as in force." [64]   Thus, as far as the court was concerned, the political departments had acted.   The question as to whether the power remains in a foreign state to carry out its treaty obligations was "in its nature political and not judicial." [65]   And as Justice Fuller declared, the "courts ought not to interfere with the conclusions of the political department . . ." [66]

The case of *Charlton* v. *Kelly* [67] concerned the extradition of an American citizen charged with the commission of murder in Italy.   The "Convention for the Extradition of Criminals, Fugitive from Justice," [68] between the United States and Italy, provided that "persons" guilty of crime in one country and fleeing to the other should be given up upon demand.   It was alleged that if the term "person," as used in the treaty, included citizens of the asylum country, then the treaty was abrogated by the action of Italy in refusing to deliver up its own citizens upon the demand of the United States.   In a memorandum [69] of Secretary Knox giving reasons for the surrender of the appellant, it was said:

The question is now for the first time presented as to whether or not the United States is under obligation under treaty to surrender to Italy for trial and punishment citizens of the United States fugitive from the justice of Italy, notwithstanding the interpretation placed upon the treaty by Italy with reference to Italian subjects. In this connection it should be observed that the United States, although as stated above, consistently contending that the Italian interpretation was not the proper one, has not treated the Italian practice as a breach of the treaty obligation necessarily requiring abrogation, has not abrogated the treaty, or taken any steps looking thereto, and has on the contrary, constantly regarded the treaty as in full force and effect . . . , [thus] the treaty is binding until abro-

---

[62] 184 U. S. 285.
[63] *Treaties and Conventions*, p. 921.
[64] 184 U. S. 285.   [66] *Ibid.*
[65] *Ibid.*, 288.   [67] 229 U. S. 447 (1913).
[68] *Treaties and Conventions*, p. 578.
[69] *Foreign Relations of the United States*, 1910, pp. 654-657.

gated, its provisions are operative against us. The question would therefore appear to reduce itself to one of interpretation of the meaning of the treaty. . . . It should be observed, in the first place, that we have always insisted not only with reference to the Italian extradition treaty, but with reference to the other extradition treaties similarly phrased, that the word " persons " includes citizens.[70]

So, based on this determination of the political department as to whether the treaty with Italy was still in force, the court concluded: " The Executive Department having thus elected to waive any right to free itself from the obligation to deliver up its own citizens, it is the plain duty of this court to recognize the obligation to surrender the appellant as one imposed by the treaty as the supreme law of the land, and as affording authority for the warrant of extradition." [71]

It has been stated as a general rule of international law that " war terminates all treaties between belligerents," [72] but, like most general rules, there are exceptions. As far as the courts of the United States are concerned, it is not international law, but the law of the Constitution, that serves as guide; war or no war, if the political departments act to terminate a treaty, that treaty may be considered as terminated; and, war or no war, if the political departments do not terminate a treaty, that treaty may be considered as still in force. Mr. Webster, arguing for New Haven in the case of the *Society for the Propagation of the Gospel in Foreign Parts* v. *New Haven*,[73] maintained that " if those rights were so protected,[74] the effect of the late war between the United States and Great Britain, was such as to put an end to those treaties, and, consequently, to rights derived under them, unless they have been revived by the treaty of peace at Ghent; which was not done." [75]

---

[70] *Ibid.*, p. 656.
[71] *Charlton* v. *Kelly*, 229 U. S. 476 (1913). See also *Johnson* v. *Gearlds*, 234 U. S. 422 (1914), and *Williams* v. *Johnson*, 239 U. S. 414 (1915).
[72] John W. Foster, *The Practice of Diplomacy*, p. 305.
[73] 8 Wheat. 464 (1823).
[74] By treaties of 1783 and 1794. See *Treaties and Conventions*, pp. 375, 379.
[75] From argument of Mr. Webster, 8 Wheat. 475-476.

Mr. Justice Washington, in delivering the opinion of the court, replied to Webster's argument as follows:

> But we are not inclined to admit the doctrine urged at the bar, that treaties become extinguished, *ipso facto*, by war between the two governments, unless they should be revived by an express or implied renewal on the return of peace. Whatever may be the latitude of the doctrine laid down by elementary writers on the law of nations, dealing in general terms in relation to this subject, we are satisfied that the doctrine contended for is not universally true. There may be treaties of such a nature, as to their object and import, as that war will put an end to them; but where treaties contemplate a permanent arrangement of territorial, and other national rights, or which, in their terms, are meant to provide for the event of an inter-vening war, it would be against every principle of just interpretation to hold them extinguished by the event of war. If such were the law, even the treaty of 1783, so far as it fixed our limits, and acknowledged our independence, would be gone, and we should have had again to struggle for both upon original revolutionary principles. . . . We think, therefore, that treaties stipulating for permanent rights, and general arrangements, and professing to aim at perpetuity, and to deal with the case of war as well as of peace, do not cease on the occurrence of war, but are, at most, only suspended while it lasts; and unless they are waived by the parties, or new and repug-nant stipulations are made, they revive in their operation at the return of peace.[76]

Here the court, seemingly extending its jurisdiction too far, decided that a particular treaty had not been terminated as the result of a state of war; and as one publicist has said, "the cases in which this has been done have been those in which there had been no action by the political departments of the government on the subject." [77]   But assuming, as in the above case, that there has been no action on the part of the political departments, the question remains: would the court be within its right to declare a treaty terminated by a state of war? It is thought not, and for two reasons: first, had the political departments declared the treaty terminated, the court would have accepted that decision and acted accord-ingly; and, secondly, since the political departments had not acted one way or another, the court could only assume that, in spite of an intervening state of war, the treaty was still in existence, it being, during the period of the war, merely suspended.[78]

---

[76] 8 Wheat. 494.
[77] Field, *Minnesota Law Review*, VIII, 489.
[78] The Treaty of Paris, 1783, may be termed an *executed* treaty

II

Turning now to the interpretation of treaties as a political question, it may be said at once that where a treaty confers private rights, such as are enforceable in a municipal court, on the citizens or subjects of the nations party to it, the courts look upon the treaty as a rule of decision and place their own interpretation upon it.[79] For example, in the case of *DeGeoffroy* v. *Riggs*,[80] the question arose as to whether a French citizen was entitled to own property in the District of Columbia by right of inheritance from an American citizen. By the terms of the treaty of 1853,[81] entered into by the United States and France, the right of a French citizen to own inherited property in the United States applied to "all the States of the Union," which apparently excluded the District. Laying down the general principle concerning treaties "that they shall be liberally construed, so as to carry out the apparent intention of the parties to secure equality and reciprocity between them," [82] the court construed the clause to be broad enough to include the District of Columbia.

But, where public rights are involved in a treaty, the courts accept the interpretation of the political departments; [83] that is, in spite of the fact that treaties operate by their own force as municipal law on terms of equality with acts of Congress, the courts, where these treaties involve external operations as an international compact, will follow the deter-

---

as distinguished from an *executory* treaty. The former, called also a transitory or dispositive treaty deals "with single acts, which are to be performed forthwith, and which, when performed, dispose of the matter once and for all. Of such character are boundary conventions and treaties of cession. . . ." Fenwick, *International Law*, p. 321. The latter type embraces treaties of commerce and extradition, treaties establishing administrative agencies, treaties of alliance, guarantee, and neutralization. But as McNair says "unanimity as to what treaties are or are not cancelled by war does not exist." Oppenheim, II, 202.

[79] That is, when the treaty is self-executing.

[80] 133 U. S. 258 (1890).

[81] *Treaties and Conventions*, p. 350.

[82] 133 U. S. 258.

[83] "So far as treaties are regarded as international compacts, the national rights and obligations accruing thereunder are determined by the political departments of the government." Willoughby, *Constitutional Law of the United States*, I, 578.

minations of the political departments, the legislative and executive, in matters of interpretation.[84]   For example, the determination of boundaries or jurisdiction over territory in accordance with treaty provisions has been held by the Supreme Court not to be within its jurisdiction.   This attitude of the court is precisely declared in the case of *Foster* v. *Neilson*.[85]   This was a suit brought by Foster to recover a certain tract of land, in the possession of the defendant, situated in the eastern district of Louisiana, three miles east of the Mississippi, claimed by grant from the Spanish governor on January 2, 1804 to Jayme Joydra, the grant having been ratified by the King of Spain on May 29, 1804.   The defendant claimed that the territory within which the disputed land was situated had been ceded, before the grant to Jayme Joydra, to France, and by France to the United States, and that therefore the grant was null and void.

At the commencement, in 1755, of the Seven Years War, France was the undisputed possessor of the province of Louisiana.   This great tract of land lay on both sides of the Mississippi and extended to the southeastward beyond the bay of Mobile to the Perdido river, which separated the French province from Florida.   At this time, Florida was in the possession of Spain.   In 1762, France, by secret treaty, ceded the Louisiana territory to Spain, but, as part of this cession, French possessions to the east of the Mississippi were not included, since, by the treaty of Paris,[86] 1763, France ceded her territory to the east of the river, with the exception of New Orleans, to Great Britain.   Twenty years later this territory was ceded to Spain.[87]   By the treaty of San Ildefonso, 1800, the King of Spain promised " to retrocede to the French Republic . . . the Province of Louisiana, with the same extent that it now has in the hands of Spain, and

---

[84] " This is, however, not an absolutely obligatory rule.   It is one of expediency. . . ."   *Ibid.*

[85] 2 Pet. 253.   This case reflected what is called the west Florida controversy.   See Isaac J. Cox, *The West Florida Controversy, 1798-1813*.

[86] *H. Doc.*, no. 121, 20th Cong., 2d sess., pp. 258-259 (extract).

[87] Traité définitif de paix et d'amitie entre S. M. Britannique et le Roi d'Espagne.   September 3, 1783.   3 Martens 541.

that it had when France possessed it. . . ." [88]   And article 2
of the treaty of Paris,[89] by which the United States acquired
the Louisiana territory, ran, in part, as follows:

> The First Consul of the French Republic desiring to give to the
> United-States a strong proof of his friendship, doth hereby cede to
> the said United-States, in the name of the French Republic, for ever
> and in full sovereignty, the said territory with all it's rights . . . as
> fully and in the same manner as they have been acquired by the
> French Republic in virtue of the above mentioned treaty, concluded
> with his Catholic Majesty.[90]

Under the latter treaty, the United States made claim to
that territory lying east of the Mississippi, between the Iberville and the Perdido rivers, and in which lay the grant, the
subject of the controversy in *Foster* v. *Neilson*.   Spain contended that her cession of Louisiana to France in 1800 included only the territory which at the time was called Louisiana, namely, the island of New Orleans and the country
received from France in 1762, west of the Mississippi.   The
difficulty lay in the ambiguity attached to the clause in the
treaty of San Ildefonso to the effect that Spain would retrocede the territory to France " with the same extent that it
now has in the hands of Spain, and that it had when France
possessed it." [91]

Whether or not Spain, by the treaty of San Ildefonso, did
include that country east of the Mississippi to the Perdido
and south of the thirty-first parallel in the cession of the
province of Louisiana to France, is a question which need
not be decided here.   For our purposes we shall accept Marshall's conclusion that " the language of the article may
admit of either construction. . . ." [92]

It will be remembered that in the case under discussion
the Supreme Court was called upon to adjudicate a controversy involving the interpretation of a treaty; but the court
did not offer its own interpretation.   " In a controversy
between two nations," said Marshall, " concerning national
boundary, it is scarcely possible that the courts of either

---

[88] *Foster* v. *Neilson*, 2 Pet. 253, 301 (1829).
[89] 7 Martens 706.   [91] 2 Pet. 301.
[90] *Ibid.*, 709.   [92] *Ibid.*, 306.

should refuse to abide by the measures adopted by its own government. There being no common tribunal to decide between them, each determines for itself on its own rights, and if they cannot adjust their differences peaceably, the right remains with the strongest. The judiciary is not that department of the government to which the assertion of its interests against foreign powers is confided. . . . If the course of the nation has been a plain one, its courts would hesitate to pronounce it erroneous. We think, then, however individuals might construe the treaty of St. Ildefonso, it is the province of the court to conform its decisions to the will of the Legislature, if that will has been clearly expressed." [93]   And the will of the legislature, thought the court, had been expressed clearly enough in the several acts passed by Congress subsequent to 1803. As an example, the limits of Louisiana were enlarged to include the disputed territory by act of Congress; [94] and when the Alabama territory was established by Congress, the territory in question was included within it. [95]   By these acts and others, [96] Congress made clear its position with regard to West Florida and to the satisfaction of the court offered an interpretation which the court accepted. " After these acts of sovereign power over the territory in dispute," said Chief Justice Marshall, " asserting the American construction of the treaty by which the government claims it, to maintain the opposite construction in its own courts would certainly be an anomaly in the history and practice of nations. If those departments which are entrusted with the foreign intercourse of the nation, which assert and maintain its interests against foreign powers, have unequivocally asserted its rights of dominion over a country of which it is in possession, and which it claims under a treaty; if the Legislature has acted on the

---

[93] *Ibid.*, 307.

[94] Joseph Story, *Public and General Statutes Passed by the Congress of the United States*, II, 1230.

[95] *Ibid.*, III, 1620.

[96] October 31, 1803. *Laws of the United States of America*, VII, 3. February 24, 1804, *ibid.*, 26; March 26, 1804, *ibid.*, 112; April, 1812, Story, II, 1230; May, 1812, *ibid.*, 1248; March, 1817, Story, III, 1620; March, 1819, *ibid.*, 1634.

construction thus asserted, it is not in its own courts that this construction is to be denied. A question like this respecting the boundaries of nations is, as has been truly said, more a political than a legal question; and in its discussion, the courts of every country must respect the pronounced will of the Legislature." [97] It is hardly necessary to say that the court decided in favor of the defendant.

In a later case, *United States* v. *Reynes*,[98] a controversy involving the treaty of San Ildefonso, the Supreme Court reiterated the position assumed in the Foster case. Whether by these treaties, said the court, " the territory south of the thirty-first degree of north latitude, and lying between the Mississippi and the Perdido, was ceded to the United States, is a question into which this court will not now inquire. The legislative and executive departments of the government have determined that the entire territory was so ceded. This court have solemnly and repeatedly declared, that this was a matter peculiarly belonging to the cognizance of those departments, and that the propriety of their determination it was not within the province of the judiciary to contravene or question." [99]

A more recent case, arising out of the treaty of peace concluded between Spain and the United States,[100] is *Pearcy* v. *Stranahan*.[101] In this case the plaintiff brought action in an attempt to recover the value of certain cigars brought from the Isle of Pines and which had been seized by the collector for the port of New York. The seizure had been made under the Dingley Act [102] of 1897 which provided for an imposition of duties on certain articles " imported from foreign countries." [103] The plaintiff contended that no duty could be imposed upon the cigars in question since the Isle of Pines was possessed by the United States and therefore domestic territory.

Article 1 [104] of the treaty of peace, provided for Spanish relinquishment of sovereignty over Cuba and the occupation

---

[97] 2 Pet. 309.
[98] 9 How. 127 (1850).
[99] *Ibid.*, 153-154.
[100] 30 *Stat. L.* 1754.
[101] 205 U. S. 257 (1907).
[102] 30 *Stat. L.* 151.
[103] *Ibid.*
[104] 30 *Stat. L.* 1755.

of the island by the United States. The second article ran as follows: " Spain cedes to the United States the island of Porto Rico and other islands now under Spanish sovereignty in the West Indies, and the island of Guam in the Marianas or Ladrones." [105]   So the question arose whether the Isle of Pines was to be deemed a part of Cuba which had been declared in the case of *Neely* v. *Henkel* [106] a foreign country within the meaning of the act of June 6, 1900,[107] the act providing for the extradition from the United States of persons guilty of crime within any foreign country or territory occupied or under the control of the United States, or whether the Isle was to be considered as embraced within article 2 of the treaty. " This inquiry," said Justice Fuller, " involves the interpretation which the political departments have put upon the treaty." [108]

By the joint resolution of April 20, 1898,[109] the United States Government disclaimed any intention of exercising control or sovereignty over Cuba except with respect to the pacification of the island. The resolution, furthermore, asserted like determination to leave the island to the control of its people as soon as pacification was an accomplished fact. And for the court, the question to be decided was the signification of the term " Cuba." " In short," said the court, " all the world knew that it (the Isle of Pines) was an integral part of Cuba, and in view of the language of the joint resolution of April 20, 1898, it seems clear that the Isle of Pines was not supposed to be one of the ' other islands ' ceded by article 2." [110]   After the Spanish had evacuated Havana on January 1, 1899, the President of the United

---

[105] *Ibid.*

[106] 180 U. S. 109. In this case the question arose as to the length of time the United States may occupy and control a certain territory, namely Cuba. " It is not competent for the judiciary," said the court, " to make any declaration upon the question of the length of time during which Cuba may be rightfully occupied and controlled by the United States in order to effect its pacification,—it being the function of the political branch of the government to determine when such occupation and control shall cease, and therefore when the troops of the United States shall be withdrawn from Cuba. . . ."

[107] 31 *Stat. L.* 656.   [109] 30 *Stat. L.* 738.

[108] 205 U. S. 265.   [110] 205 U. S. 266.

States ordered a census to be taken for the purpose of assist-
ing the Cubans in establishing an effective self-government,
and in accomplishing this design the Isle of Pines was included as a municipal district of the province of Havana.[111]
In August, 1899, the military governor of Cuba appointed a
mayor of the Isle of Pines. In the election of municipal
officers, June 16, 1900, the inhabitants of the Isle partici-
pated. When a constitutional convention was called, the
voters of the Isle of Pines sent delegates. Furthermore, when
the military control of Cuba by the United States ceased,
and the government of the island was transferred to the
Cubans (May 20, 1902), the military governor, in a communication to the President and Congress of Cuba, among
other things, said: " It is understood by the United States
that the present government of the Isle of Pines will continue as a *de facto* government, pending settlement of the
title to said island by treaty. . . ."[112] It was evident that
the Isle of Pines was, and always had been, considered an
integral part of Cuba. Yet by the terms of the Platt Amendment[113] of March 2, 1901, it was provided that " the Isle
of Pines shall be omitted from the proposed constitutional
boundaries of Cuba, the title thereto being left to future
adjustment by treaty."[114]

With a view to settling the question of the Isle of Pines,
the United States on July 2, 1903, negotiated a treaty with
Cuba by which the former relinquished all claims to the Isle
under the treaty of peace with Spain. But this failed of
ratification. In the following year, on March 2, 1904, another
treaty to the same effect was signed, but, at the time of
Pearcy v. *Stranahan,* the treaty had not been ratified; in fact,
it was not until March 13, 1925, that the treaty was at last
ratified.[115]

Thus, the interpretation which the political departments
had put upon articles 1 and 2 of the treaty with Spain was
none too clear. " It may be conceded," said the court, " that

---

[111] *Ibid.*, 266-267.
[112] *Ibid.*, 268.
[113] 31 *Stat. L.* 895.
[114] *Ibid.*, 898.
[115] See *New York Times*, March 14, 1925.

the action of both the political departments has not been
sufficiently definite to furnish a conclusive interpretation of
the treaty of peace as an original question, and as yet no
agreement has been reached under the Platt amendment.
The Isle of Pines continues, at least *de facto,* under the
jurisdiction . . . of the Republic of Cuba, and that settles
the question before us, because, as the United States have
never taken possession of the Isle of Pines as having been
ceded by the treaty of peace, and as it has been and is being
governed by the Republic of Cuba, it has remained 'foreign
country' within the meaning of the Dingley act. . . ." [116]

III

It will be remembered in the case of *Foster* v. *Neilson,*[117]
discussed above, that the United States assumed the position
that to her belonged the territory lying between the Iberville
and the Perdido rivers, and the Supreme Court sustained
this contention by declaring the question as to whether or
not the territory concerned was within the jurisdiction of
the United States to be political. As the cases clearly indicate, where the question of jurisdiction over territory has
arisen, whether the territory be claimed by the United States
or not, the Supreme Court accepts and applies the attitude
of the political departments.

A comparatively recent case in which the question arose
was *Wilson* v. *Shaw,*[118] a controversy in which the plaintiff
invoked the assistance of the courts to prevent the Government of the United States from constructing the Panama
Canal. It is little wonder that Mr. Justice Brewer thought

---

[116] 205 U. S. 272.

[117] 2 Pet. 253 (1829). The doctrine of political questions likewise
applies to disputed territory involving Indian lands. A case in
point is *Latimer* v. *Poteet,* 14 Pet. 4 (1840). Here Justice M'Lean
stated that "it is a sound principle of national law, and applies to
the treaty-making power of this government, whether exercised with
a foreign nation or an Indian tribe, that all questions of disputed
boundaries may be settled by the parties to the treaty. And to the
exercise of these high functions by the government, within its constitutional power, neither the rights of a State nor those of an
individual can be interposed."

[118] 204 U. S. 24 (1907).

the magnitude of the plaintiff's demand somewhat startling. The plaintiff argued first that " whatever title the government has was not acquired as provided in the act of June 28, 1902,[119] by treaty with the Republic of Columbia." [120] To this contention, Justice Brewer said:

A short but sufficient answer is that subsequent ratification is equivalent to original authority. The title to what may be called the Isthmian or canal zone, which at the date of the act, was in the Republic of Columbia, passed by an act of secession to the newly formed Republic of Panama. The latter was recognized as a nation by the President. A treaty with it, ceding the canal zone, was duly ratified.[121] Congress has passed several acts based upon the title of the United States, among them one to provide a temporary government; [122] another, fixing the status of merchandise coming into the United States from the canal zone; [123] another prescribing the type of canal.[124] These show a full ratification by Congress of what has been done by the Executive. This concurrent action is conclusive upon the courts. We have not supervising control over the political branch of the government in its action within the limits of the Constitution.[125]

Since the method of acquisition was found by the plaintiff to be faulty, he was next led to the proposition that the United States had no power to construct a canal in Panama and based his contention on the notion that the Canal Zone was not a part of the territory of the United States. But this proposition, in the light of articles 2 [126] and 3 [127] of the

---

[119] 32 *Stat. L.* 481.   [122] *Ibid.*, 429.
[120] 204 U. S. 32.   [123] *Ibid.*, 843.
[121] 33 *Stat. L.* 2234.   [124] 34 *Stat. L.* 611.

[125] 204 U. S. 32. A supervising control, however, is indicated in *Fleming* v. *Page*, 9 How. 603 (1850). Here the question arose whether during the control of Tampico by the United States military and naval forces, Tampico was to be considered as part of the United States. The United States, said Taney, " may extend its boundaries by conquest or treaty, and may demand the cession of territory as the condition of peace. . . . But this can be done only by the treaty-making power or the legislative authority, and is not a part of the power conferred upon the President by the declaration of war." *Ibid.*, 614-615. Later in the opinion he said with reference to the territory in question, " after it was subdued, it was uniformly treated as an enemy's country, and restored to the possession of the Mexican authorities when peace was concluded. And certainly its subjugation did not compel the United States, while they held it, to regard it as a part of their dominions. . . ." *Ibid.*, 618.

[126] 33 *Stat. L.* 2234-2235. " The Republic of Panama grants to the United States in perpetuity the use, occupation and control of a zone of land and land under water for the construction, maintenance, operation, sanitation and protection of said Canal. . . ."

[127] *Ibid.*, 2235. " The Republic of Panama grants to the United

Isthmian Canal Convention, was held by the court to be
false. To the court, the political departments, by treaty and
by act of Congress, had shown conclusively that the United
States Government claimed and maintained jurisdiction over
the Canal Zone, and for the court, this was enough.

O. P. Field, in the aforementioned article dealing with
political questions, says that " not only does the rule . . .
apply to the assertion of jurisdiction over land, but it also
applies to the sea. Nations sometimes assert a jurisdiction
over the sea extending far beyond the three-mile limit which
has up to the present time generally been considered the
usual extent of national jurisdiction. The United States has
been guilty of just this sort of thing, and the courts have in
several cases been forced to abide by the assertion of such
jurisdiction by Congress." [128] The law of nations holds such
extended jurisdiction by one nation to be a violation of the
doctrine of the freedom of the seas, excluding, of course,
territorial waters, straits, gulfs and bays, which are parts
of the sea, but not of the " open sea." [129] The maritime belt
supposedly extends but three miles, allegedly the range of
an early eighteenth-century cannon, from the shore. However, from the point of view of constitutional law, that is,
juristically speaking, the United States could, without regard
to the principles of international law, claim and attempt to
maintain a jurisdiction extending many leagues beyond the
three-mile limit; and such a claim of the government would
be upheld by the courts.

For particular purposes, the government of the United
States has claimed jurisdiction over the open sea. By the
treaty of March 30, 1867,[130] between Russia and the United
States, the former ceded to the latter, in return for a certain

States all the rights, power and authority within the zone mentioned
and described in article 2 of this agreement and within the limits of
all auxiliary lands and waters mentioned and described in said article
2 which the United States would possess and exercise if it were the
sovereign of the territory within which said land and waters are
located to the entire exclusion of the exercise by the Republic of
Panama of any such sovereign rights, power or authority."
[128] *Minnesota Law Review*, VIII, 497.
[129] See Oppenheim, pp. 475 ff.
[130] *Treaties and Conventions*, p. 939.

sum of money, the territory of Alaska and other of her possessions in North America, besides all the Russian rights of trade and navigation in the Behring Sea, which were extensive to say the least. Article 1 set the western limit of the cession as a line of division running practically midway through the Behring Sea in a north-south direction.[131]   In the following year, 1868, Congress, not specifying the extent of the territory ceded to the United States, simply provided among other things that " the laws of the United States relating to customs, commerce, and navigation be, and the same are hereby, extended to and over all the mainland, islands, and waters of the territory ceded to the United States " [132] by Russia; and provided furthermore, that " it shall be unlawful for any person or persons to kill any otter, mink, marten, sable, or fur seal, or other fur-bearing animal, within the limits of said territory, or in the waters thereof. . . ." [133]

After the acquisition of this territory, the salmon fisheries and the hunting of fur-bearing animals as a business developed rapidly in the waters about Alaska; to such magnitude, in fact, that with special reference to the latter, it was thought that in no very far off time, this important source of furs would be destroyed. As a consequence, the government took active measures to limit the capture of seals, primarily by assuming jurisdiction over that part of the Behring Sea bounded on the west by the aforementioned imaginary line, and declaring with reference to seal hunting, that part of the sea, a *mare clausum*.[134]   However, the evils of pelagic fishing did not diminish, poaching continued, and the government felt constrained to send revenue cutters to the scene. In 1886, three British vessels " out for seal " were captured beyond the three-mile limit, and later condemned in a United States court; and during the following summer several more

---

[131] *Ibid.*, pp. 939-940.
[132] 15 *Stat. L.* 240.   [133] *Ibid.*, 241.
[134] "All the waters within that boundary to the western end of the Aleutian Archipelago and chain of islands are considered as comprised within the waters of Alaska territory." From a letter of Mr. French, acting secretary of the Treasury, March 12, 1881, to D. A. d'Ancona, Collector of the port of San Francisco. Quoted in J. B. Henderson, *American Diplomatic Questions*, p. 15.

were captured, among them the "W. P. Sawyard." This gave rise to the case of *In re Cooper*.[135]

The facts of the case were simple. The schooner, " W. P. Sawyard," owned by one Cooper, was captured by a United States revenue cutter, fifty-nine miles from any land whatsoever. Cooper was charged with having hunted and killed seals in violation of an act of Congress. The vessel was carried to Sitka where it was delivered to the United States marshal, libelled in the district court, and condemned. Cooper then made application to the Supreme Court of the United States for a writ of prohibition [136] to restrain the enforcement of a sentence of forfeiture and condemnation on the ground that the United States did not have jurisdiction over half of the Behring Sea.

The court, in *In re Cooper,* considered itself bound by the action of the political departments in claiming jurisdiction over the Behring Sea, extending at least fifty-nine miles from the Alaskan mainland.

And it is insisted that when Congress in section 1956 speaks of 'Alaska Territory' and 'the waters thereof,' it could only mean, so far as the sea was concerned, three miles . . . from the shore of the continent, or from the shores of one of the adjacent islands, and that the act of March 2, 1889,[137] does not in any way enlarge the effect of section 1956, because 'the dominion of the United States in the waters of the Behring sea' is limited by the law of nations to the distance from the shore above mentioned. If we assume that the record shows the locality of the alleged offence and seizure as stated, it also shows that officers of the United States, acting under the orders of their government, seized this vessel engaged in catching seal and took her into the nearest port; and that the law officers of the government libelled her and proceeded against her for the violation of the laws of the United States, in the District Court, resulting in her condemnation.

Justice Fuller continued,

How did it happen that the officers received such orders? It must be admitted that they were given in the assertion on the part of this government of territorial jurisdiction over Behring sea to an extent exceeding fifty-nine miles from the shores of Alaska; that this territorial jurisdiction, in the enforcement of the laws protecting

---

[135] 143 U. S. 472 (1892).

[136] This is a common law writ which lies to an inferior court when that court is acting in excess of, or is taking cognizance of, matters not within its jurisdiction.

[137] 25 *Stat. L.* (50th Cong., 2d sess.) ch. 415.

seal fisheries, was asserted by actual seizures during the seasons of 1886, 1887 and 1889 of a number of British vessels; that the government persistently maintains that such jurisdiction belongs to it, based not only on the peculiar nature of the seal fisheries and the property of the government in them, but also upon the position that this jurisdiction was asserted by Russia [138] for more than ninety years, and by that government transferred to the United States.[139]

On the ground that the United States had claimed jurisdiction over that part of the Behring Sea, the court held that the district court for Alaska did have jurisdiction of the case, and so denied the writ of prohibition.

The Supreme Court has also held that the determination of which of two foreign nations is sovereign over a certain territory rests with the political departments. A case in point is *Williams* v. *Suffolk Insurance Company.*[140] This controversy concerned a vessel, insured by the Suffolk Company, which was seized and condemned at the Falkland Islands, allegedly under the sovereignty and within the jurisdiction of the government of Buenos Aires. The plaintiff brought action in order to recover a loss on the schooner and part of her cargo which had been insured by the defendant company. The insurance company had refused to pay the insurance, claiming that the master of the vessel had fished in the territorial waters of a foreign nation in violation of the law of Buenos Aires, and the terms of the insurance policy.

In expressing the opinion of the court, Mr. Justice M'Lean said:

And can there be any doubt that when the executive branch of the government, which is charged with our foreign relations, shall in its correspondence with a foreign nation assume a fact in regard to the sovereignty of any island or country, it is conclusive on the judicial department? And in this view it is not material to inquire, nor is it the province of the court to determine, whether the executive be right or wrong. It is enough to know that in the exercise of his constitutional functions he has decided the question. Having done this under the responsibilities which belong to him, it is obligatory on the people and government of the Union.[141]

Thus, with respect to the case, Justice M'Lean continued: " we think in the present case, as the executive, in his mes-

---

[138] See F. Snow, *Treaties and Topics in American Diplomacy,* p. 472.
[139] 143 U. S. 498-499.   [140] 13 Pet. 415 (1839).   [141] *Ibid.,* 420.

sage, and in his correspondence with the government of Buenos Ayres, has denied the jurisdiction which it has assumed to exercise over the Falkland Islands; the fact must be taken and acted on by this court as thus asserted and maintained." [142] Since it was discovered that the master of the vessel had not violated the law of Buenos Aires, there being none so far as concerned the court, in fishing in the waters about the Falkland Islands, it was evident that he had not violated the terms of the insurance policy, and that the company was still liable.

Here, again, we find a practical element operating as an essential reason for placing the question of jurisdiction in the category of political questions. As to the problem of foreign jurisdiction raised in this case, if the doctrine did not apply, irreconcilable differences between executive and judiciary might arise and lead only to confusion. The executive might consider a foreign nation to be sovereign over a certain territory, while the court might accept a diametrically opposite point of view, and as Justice M'Lean pointed out, "no well regulated government has ever sanctioned a principle so unwise, so destructive of national character." [143]

If the court leaves to the political departments the right of deciding whether a certain territory is under the jurisdiction of the United States or of a foreign nation, it seems only logical that the date of the acquisition of such territory by the United States would be left, not for the judiciary, but for the executive and legislative departments to decide. In the case of *United States* v. *Pico*, [144] which involved the title of a Mexican to land in California, subsequent to the conquest, and dependent for its decision upon the commencement of the jurisdiction of the United States over that territory, Mr. Justice Campbell speaking for the court said: "In the Act of Congress of 1851,[145] and the decisions of this court, that day (July 7, 1846; the date of the capture of Monterey) is referred to as the epoch at which the power of the Governor of California, under the authority of Mexico, to

---

[142] *Ibid.*   [143] *Ibid.*   [144] 23 How. 321 (1860).
[145] 9 *Stat. L.* 631.

alienate the public domain, terminated." [146]   In another case, also centering around the termination of Mexican jurisdiction over California, it was said that "the authority and jurisdiction of Mexican officials are regarded as terminating on the 7th of July, 1846; on that day the forces of the United States took possession of Monterey, an important town in California, and within a few weeks afterwards occupied the principal portions of the country, and the military occupation continued until the Treaty of Peace.[147]   The Political Department of the Government at least appears to have designated that day as the period when the conquest of California was completed, and the Mexican officials were displaced; and in this respect the Judiciary follows the action of the Political Department." [148]

So far, we have reviewed cases indicating the dependence of the courts upon the political departments in the determination as to the jurisdiction of the United States over territory, the jurisdiction assumed or claimed over a particular territory by two foreign nations, and the date as to when a territory falls under the jurisdiction of the United States. There are, however, various ramifications of the same doctrine, involving jurisdiction, which may well be discussed here. For instance, it was held by the Supreme Court in the case of *Phillips* v. *Payne*,[149] that it could not determine the validity of the retrocession of territory by the United States to a state of the Union. In 1789, subsequent to the establishment of the Union, Virginia ceded to the national government a part of her territory bordering the Potomac, to constitute, with a similar cession from Maryland, what is known as the District of Columbia. The Congress accepted the cessions. However, in 1846, Congress passed an act [150] authorizing the people of Alexandria county, then a part of the District of Columbia, to vote either to maintain the *status quo,* or to retrocede the county back to the State of Virginia. A majority of votes were cast for retrocession; and since, according to the act of 1846, all rights and jurisdiction

---

[146] 23 How. 326.   [147] *Treaties and Conventions*, p. 681.

[148] *United States* v. *Yorba*, 1 Wall. 412 (1864).

[149] 92 U. S. 130 (1876).   [150] Story, V, 3107.

were to be "ceded and forever relinquished to the State of Virginia," [151] without any action on the part of Congress, the State of Virginia passed an Act declaring that the county was re-annexed, and formed a part of the State." [152]

The suit was brought by the plaintiff-in-error to recover back taxes from a collector of the State of Virginia, and he raised the question as to whether the retrocession of the territory by Congress to the State of Virginia was valid and legal. At the conclusion of the opinion of the majority in this case it was said that "the plaintiff in error is estopped from raising the point which he seeks to have decided. He cannot, under the circumstances, vicariously raise a question, nor force upon the parties [153] to the compact an issue which neither of them desires to make. In this litigation we are constrained to regard the *de facto* condition of things which exists with reference to the County of Alexandria as conclusive of the rights of the parties before us." [154]

The determination of the boundaries of a military reservation, also has been held by the court to be a political question. A case in point is *Benson* v. *United States*,[155] in which Benson, the plaintiff-in-error, was convicted in the circuit court of the United States for the district of Kansas, for murder and sentenced to be hanged. It was alleged by counsel for the government that the crime had been committed on the Leavenworth military reservation; while, on the other hand, Benson contended that "jurisdiction passed to the general government only over such portions of the reserve as are actually used for military purposes, and that the particular part of the reserve on which the crime charged was committed was used solely for farming purposes." [156] In few words, the contention of the plaintiff was that the United States courts had no jurisdiction over the case.

---

[151] *Ibid.*   [152] 92 U. S. 130.

[153] The United States Government and the State of Virginia.

[154] 92 U. S. 130. It was further said that "the political departments of her (Virginia's) government, by their conduct, have uniformly asserted her title; and the head of her judicial department has expressly affirmed it. . . . The United States have not objected. . . . Congress, by more than one Act, has recognized the transfer as a settled and valid fact."

[155] 146 U. S. 325 (1892).   [156] *Ibid.*

To this, however, the court attached no weight.   In matters of this sort, said Justice Brewer, " the courts follow the action of the political department of the government.   The entire tract had been legally reserved for military purposes. The character and purposes of its occupation having been officially and legally established by that branch of the government which has control over such matters, it is not open to the courts, on a question of jurisdiction, to inquire what may be the actual uses to which any portion of the reserve is temporarily put.   There was therefore jurisdiction in the circuit court. . . ." [157]

The course of our journey among the most significant cases involving political questions has come, at last, to a turning point.   Out of the various cases, whether the question involved be the legal status of Indian tribes, which of two contending governmental organizations within a state of the Union is the *de jure* government, the questions of jurisdiction over territory, or the recognition of states and governments, one fact emerges sharply, and that is the legal effect of denominating such questions " political questions."   Whenever a court invokes the doctrine of political questions, such invocation inevitably excludes the question, to which the doctrine is applied, from the category of justiciable controversies.   The courts wash their hands of such questions and accept the decisions of the political departments with regard to them.

But there is more to political questions than this.   So far, we have observed the legal effect when a question is labelled " political."   We must yet discover *why* the courts make use of the doctrine; *why* the courts label these questions " political questions."

---

[157] *Ibid.*   However, the Supreme Court has jurisdiction over boundary disputes between states of the Union.   See *Rhode Island* v. *Massachusetts*, 12 Pet. 657 (1838).   Likewise a controversy between the United States and a state of the Union concerning the boundary of a state and an adjoining territory of the United States may be settled by the Supreme Court.   In the case of *United States* v. *State of Texas*, 143 U. S. 621 (1892), it was held that such a question is not a political one; that by virtue of art. 3, sec. 2, of the Constitution, the judicial power extends to such controversies.

CHAPTER IV

" POLITICAL QUESTIONS " AS A CATEGORY OF THE JUDICIAL THOUGHT-PROCESS

In approaching the question why jurists place certain prob-lems in the category of political questions the writer is filled with trepidation. It is comparatively easy to observe how people act; we can see a man hoeing his garden, spanking a child, or drinking intoxicating liquors. But if we ask why the man hoes his garden, spanks the child, or drinks an alcoholic beverage, we at once enter the labyrinthine snare of the Minotaur. The man hoes his garden, but does he do so because of needed exercise, or because he and his family are in dire need of the products hoped for; the man spanks the child, but is it because of his ungovernable temper or because the child has been extremely naughty and is perhaps deserving of the whipping; we see a man drinking, but does he do so because he enjoys what he is imbibing, or because he wants to ward off a chill, or because he wishes to forget himself and the world of actuality? It is the same with political questions. We can observe, or be conscious of, the fact that when the court denominates a problem a political question it generally leaves the problem to be decided by the political departments. A more difficult question is why the courts place a question in the category.

A recent publicist has found that the courts cannot decide certain questions because " where no rules exist the court is powerless to act," [1] and that such questions are labelled by the court, " political questions." One cannot, without diffi-culty, subscribe to this point of view. In the case of *McCul-loch* v. *Maryland*,[2] the Supreme Court was faced with the ques-tion whether the Federal government was entitled to charter a bank and authorize the establishment of branches in the several states. The Constitution did not give Congress the express power to charter banks. Had Chief Justice Marshall

---

[1] Field, *Minnesota Law Review*, VIII, 511.
[2] 4 Wheat. 316 (1819).

been rigidly dependent upon rules he might have been in the position of the Vermont justice of the peace "before whom a suit was brought by one farmer against another for breaking a churn. The justice took time to consider, and then said that he had looked through the statutes and could find nothing about churns, and gave judgment for the defendant." [3] There were no explicit rules for the court to follow in determining whether Congress had the right to establish a bank, and yet the court declared such establishment to be constitutional. It would seem that the court made its own rules. And if, as Professor Field says, "the courts cannot enter into questions of statecraft or policy," [4] how is it that the Supreme Court in this case actually decided a question, which to the present writer at least, might well be deemed a matter of policy; and if this be admitted, could it not properly be argued that such a question belonged in the category of political questions and that the court should never have decided the question in the first place? It is only submitted here that the writer is not at all clear as to what is meant by the terms "statecraft or policy" as used by Professor Field.

The Federal courts, and particularly the Supreme Court, have seldom, during the course of their history, assumed an attitude of impotence. "The most spectacular crisis in intellectual history since Darwin's *Origin of Species*," says Professor Dickinson, "has come with the challenge which Einstein and the modern physicists have flung down to the Newtonian conception of nature. Like its Darwinian predecessor this more recent crisis has sent waves of repercussion

---

[3] Oliver W. Holmes, "The Path of the Law," *Harvard Law Review*, X, 474.

[4] Field, p. 511. As a matter of fact, Professor Field includes the power of Congress to exclude and expel aliens in the category of political questions. To be sure, the attitude of the National government with respect to aliens is a matter of "policy" which the courts accept in deciding cases. But the power to exclude and expel is as frankly a legislative power as the power of Congress to tax and to regulate foreign commerce, both of which, in their exercise, express a "policy." If, therefore, the question of the exclusion and expulsion of aliens is to be denominated a political question, it would seem that, likewise, the power of the Federal government to tax and to regulate commerce should be placed in the same category.

into other fields of thought; and arriving within the domain of jurisprudence, the impact has struck amidships not merely the idea of law as a system of logically connected rules, but even the more fundamental idea of rules as controlling factors in the process of decision." [5] What is more, Professor Dickinson declares that the actual " decision of any litigated controversy results almost always from the determination of numerous issues, on many of which there is not, and on some of which there cannot ever be, a controlling rule of law." [6] To take a concrete case, in *Hynes* v. *New York Central Railroad Company*,[7] as a boy poised himself on a spring board to dive into the Hudson River, electric wires belonging to the railroad company fell and struck him, thereby causing his death. " In the suit for damages that followed," says Mr. Justice Cardozo who rendered the opinion in the case, " competitive analogies were invoked by counsel for the administratrix and counsel for the railroad company, the owner of the upland. The administratrix found the analogy that suited her in the position of travelers on the highway. The boy was a bather in navigable waters; his rights were not lessened because his feet were on the board. The owner found the analogy to its liking in the position of a trespasser on land. The spring board, though it projected into the water, was, none the less, a fixture, and as a fixture it was constructively a part of the land to which it was annexed. The boy was thus a trespasser upon land in private ownership, hence the only duty of the owner was to refrain from wanton and malicious injury. If these elements were lacking, the death must go without requital. Now," continues Justice Cardozo, " the truth is that, as a mere bit of dialectics, these analogies would bring a judge to an impasse. No process of merely logical deduction could determine the choice between them. Neither analogy is precise, though each is apposite. There had arisen a new situation which could not force itself without mutilation into any of the existing

---

[5] John Dickinson, " Legal Rules: Their Function in the Process of Decision," *University of Pennsylvania Law Review*, LXXIX, 834.
[6] *Ibid.*, p. 835.　　　　　　　　[7] 231 N. Y. 229 (1921).

moulds. When we find a situation of this kind, the choice that will approve itself to this judge or to that, will be determined largely by his conception of the end of the law, the function of legal liability; and this question of ends and functions is a question of philosophy." [8] It is evident that there was no controlling rule of law to apply specifically to the particular set of facts. If we accede to the view that " where no rules exist the court is powerless to act," how is it that the court in the Hynes case rendered a decision?

Let us examine, for a moment, another interesting case, *Oppenheim* v. *Kridel*.[9] Previous to the decision in this case the law said or implied that no woman could entertain a suit for criminal conversation except with the connivance of her husband, and a lower court in *Oppenheim* v. *Kridel* had so decided it; but, fortunately, for the plaintiff, on appeal her case was reviewed by Judge Cardozo.

To make out the woman's disability, precedents were cited from the time of Lord Coke. Stress was laid upon pronouncements in those days that a man had a property right in the body of his wife. A wife, it was said, had none in the body of her husband. Stress was laid also upon rulings made in days when the wife was unable, unless the husband joined with her as plaintiff, to sue for any wrong. We did not ignore these precedents, but we held them inconclusive. Social, political, and legal reforms had changed the relations between the sexes, and put woman and man upon a plane of equality. Decisions founded upon the assumption of a bygone inequality were unrelated to present-day realities, and ought not to be permitted to prescribe a rule of life.[10]

A new rule was certainly created in this case.

Exceptional jurists are not afraid of rules, nor a lack of them. When necessary and for particular purposes, where no rules exist, judges will make their own rules. As Judge Cuthbert W. Pound said as recently as 1927, " we may as well disregard the overwhelming weight of authority elsewhere and start with a rule of our own, consistent with practical experience." [11] When a jurist is confronted with a new case, that is, a case in which the set-up of the facts does not

---

[8] Benjamin N. Cardozo, *The Growth of the Law*, pp. 99 ff.
[9] 236 N. Y. 156 (1923).
[10] Cardozo, pp. 105-106.
[11] *Campbell* v. *New York Evening Post*, 157 N. E. 156 (1927).

adjust itself to the known moulds, " it is obvious that he must legislate, whether he will or no. By this is meant that since he is free so far as compelling logical reasons are concerned to choose which way to decide the case, his choice will turn out upon analysis to be based upon considerations of social or economic policy. An intelligent choice can be made only by estimating as far as that is possible the consequences of a decision one way or the other." [12]

Earlier in this work we referred to the hoary and venerable doctrine of the separation of powers. It will be remembered that the Constitution specifically provides that " all legislative power herein granted shall be vested in a Congress," and with the exception of those checks and balances such as the presidential veto, one might assume that the clause means exactly what it says; that is, we might be led to that conception of the legislature as the *sole* law-making organ of government. This picture, so scorned by Mr. Jerome Frank, would present the law as " a complete body of rules existing from time immemorial and unchangeable except to the limited extent that legislatures have changed the rules by enacted statutes. Legislatures are expressly empowered thus to change the law. But the judges are not to make or change the law but to apply it. The law, ready-made, pre-exists the judicial decisions." [13] In keeping with this conception of the legislature and the judiciary, were a jurist to create law he would be guilty not only of a usurpation of power and a violation of the doctrine of the separation of powers, but of unconstitutionalism. Orthodox upholders of the doctrine would see the judges as mere robots.

Nevertheless, as we have seen in the foregoing, judges do make law. And this applies in England as well as in the United States. So eminent a publicist as Dicey, has said that " judge-made law is real law, though made under the form of, and often described, by judges no less than by jurists, as the mere interpretation of the law. Whoever

---

[12] Walter W. Cook, " Scientific Method and the Law," *Johns Hopkins Alumni Magazine*, XV, 231.
[13] Jerome Frank, *Law and the Modern Mind*, p. 32.

fairly considers how large are the masses of English law for which no other authority than judicial decisions or reported cases can be found, will easily acquiesce in the statement that law made by the judges is as truly law as are laws made by Parliament." [14]

It would seem at the present time that there exist two extreme conceptions of the judicio-legislative relation. One is that the judges have no hand in legislation at all. The other is that judges alone make the law. " The true view, as I submit," says Gray, " is that the law is what judges declare; that statutes, precedents, the opinions of learned experts, customs and morality are the sources of the law." [15] However, Mr. Justice Cardozo drives a middle course between the two extremes. He sees, on the one hand, that in " countless litigations, the law is so clear that judges have no discretion," [16] and on the other, where the law is unsettled, a duty may be cast " upon the courts to declare it retrospectively in the exercise of a power frankly legislative in function." [17]

What the writer wishes to point out here is that a " dearth of rules " and the doctrine of the separation of powers afford an unsatisfactory and unrealistic impetus to the courts when they declare a certain matter to be a political question. The Supreme Court is not powerless to act because of a lack of rules, and the separation of powers theory will not deter the court from extending its jurisdiction into conventionally nonjusticiable fields. Why, it may be asked, did the Supreme Court in *Luther* v. *Borden* abide by the decision of the political departments, while in *Texas* v. *White* it decided that the government of Texas could sue before the court when Congress had specifically declared in the Reconstruction Acts that no legal governments existed in any of the previously rebellious states?

One other explanation of political questions deserves atten-

---

[14] Albert V. Dicey, *Lectures on the Relation between Laws and Public Opinion in England during the Nineteenth Century*, p. 488.

[15] John C. Gray, *Nature and Sources of the Law*, sec. 602.

[16] *The Nature of the Judicial Process*, p. 129.

[17] *Ibid.*, p. 128.

tion. In his dissenting opinion in *Luther* v. *Borden,* Mr. Justice Woodbury maintained that "this court can never with propriety be called on officially to be the umpire in questions merely political. The adjustment of these questions belongs to the people and their political representatives, either in the State or general government." [18] If, in using the term " State " a state of the Union is meant, then Justice Woodbury seems to have forgotten that the question of the validity of a particular state government established under a particular constitution may well become the business, not alone of the people and their representatives in that particular state, but the business of the senators and representatives of (at present) forty-seven other states, and this because, first, under the Constitution of the United States, the Senate and the House decide upon the qualifications of their own members; and second, because by virtue of Article 4, section 4, of the Constitution, the United States " shall guarantee to every State in this Union a republican form of government. . . ." As for the voice of the " people " in such questions, if Congress, or, as it may be, the President, in order to determine whether or not a state government is republican in form, must decide whether it is a legal government, actually what part does the electorate play in deciding the question? It is difficult to perceive the voice of the electorate in the decision of political questions generally. The Supreme Court has repeatedly stated that the questions of the dates of the beginning and ending of war, are political, as well as the existence of a state of war, yet the electorate has nothing to do with their determination. In what respect, it may be asked, does the electorate partake of the determination of the validity of treaties or their interpretation?

All this relates only to the legal powers of the electorate. Actually, of course, the electorate might play an important, although indirect, part in determining such questions. A prevailing sentiment as expressed by press and radio (if the press and radio reflect a prevailing sentiment) opposed to

---

[18] 7 How. 51 (1849).

foreign war or the recognition of a particular government, would not be lightly ignored by the Congress or the President. The so-called "Peace Amendment," introduced in the House of Representatives on February 14, 1935, if adopted, would, however, give the electorate some legal power over the question of the existence of a state of war. This proposed amendment provides, in part, that "except in the event of an invasion of the United States or its Territorial possessions and attack upon its citizens residing therein, the authority of Congress to declare war shall not become effective until confirmed by a majority of all votes cast thereon in a Nation-wide referendum." [19]

It seems not unreasonable to conclude, therefore, that when the Supreme Court refuses to decide a question which it denominates "political," the action of the court is not so directed because of a lack of rules which binds its hands, or because such questions are to be decided by the electorate, or finally, because under the doctrine of the separation of powers the decision of such questions falls within the jurisdiction of the political departments; none of these *raisons d'être,* it would seem, afford a satisfactory explanation. However, it is not the intention of the writer carelessly to discard the doctrine of the separation of powers. Like the doctrine of political questions, it affords a very useful concept in deciding cases. The courts, time and again, have utilized the separation of powers to supply the theoretical basis of political questions; but this foundation, though useful, is misleading and unrealistic. Perhaps we shall find that when a jurist places a question in the category of political questions, his decision to do so may "turn out upon analysis to be based upon considerations of social or economic policy," [20] or expediency. Perhaps the judge is prompted to utilize the doctrine in order to attain certain consequences which he deems desirable. Perhaps a further examination of the cases will bring to light more varied aspects of the problem.

To refer again to the case of *Luther* v. *Borden* [21] it will

---

[19] *Cong. Rec.*, 74th Cong., 2d sess., p. 10,827.
[20] Cook, XV, 231.   [21] 7 How. 1.

be remembered that the Dorr Rebellion, which occurred in 1841, lasted but a few months.

Early in 1842 the Charter government called a convention to revise the then existing form of government with the result that a new constitution [22] was created—a more liberal instrument than its predecessor, the Charter of 1663. This new constitution was submitted to the people for approval in November, 1842, at which time it was ratified by an overwhelming majority.[23] In the following year it went into operation. In 1849, the constitution of 1842 was still in operation. Now, approximately eight years after the rebellion, the Supreme Court was called upon by counsel for the plaintiff in *Luther* v. *Borden* to declare that the old Charter government at the time of the insurrection, and subsequently, was not the *de jure* government, and that all of its acts, including the calling of the constitutional convention in 1842, were illegal. Let us, for the moment, suppose that the doctrine of political questions played no part in our constitutional law, and that if the court so willed, it could have, of itself, determined which of the two opposing governments was the *de jure* one. Here Chief Justice Taney permits us a glimpse of what was in the back of his mind; a glimpse of certain consequences he wished to avoid, and, by implication, the consequences he sought to achieve as desirable.

If this court is authorized to enter upon this inquiry as proposed by the plaintiff, and it should be decided that the charter government had no legal existence during the period of time above mentioned—if it had been annulled by the adoption of the opposing government— then the laws passed by its Legislature during that time were nullities; and its taxes wrongfully collected; its salaries and compensation to its officers illegally paid; its public accounts improperly settled; and the judgments and sentences of its courts in civil and criminal cases null and void, and the officers who carried their decisions into operation answerable as trespassers, if not in some cases as criminals.[24]

Taney's mind revolted at such confusion: " When the decision of this court might lead to such results, it becomes

---

[22] Poore, *Federal and State Constitutions*, II, 1605.
[23] *Ibid.*, footnote. 7,032 against 59 votes.
[24] 7 How. 38-39.

its duty to examine very carefully its own powers before it undertakes to exercise jurisdiction." [25]

With this in mind it may not be improper to suggest that Taney and his associates wished to avoid the confusion described, a confusion which would certainly have engendered countless conflicts in the courts. Furthermore, a decision that the Dorr government was the legal government would have disrupted and nullified the work of the government established under the Constitution of 1842, which, at the time the case was reviewed by the Supreme Court, had been in existence for eight years, and, throughout this period, electing and sending representatives and senators to the national Congress. It may not be improper, also, to intimate that Taney and his associates arrived at such a conclusion before they applied to rules of law; and that the whole problem was placed in the category of " political questions " in order to uphold the conclusion and to attain certain consequences. In other words, there were certain practical considerations uppermost in the minds of the jurists, and the legal bases for these practical considerations were conveniently found in the concept of the separation of powers. In conclusion, Chief Justice Taney said:

> The high power has been conferred on this court of passing judgment upon the acts of the State sovereignties, and of the legislative and executive branches of the Federal government, and of determining whether they are beyond the limits of power marked out for them respectively by the Constitution of the United States. This tribunal, therefore, should be the last to overstep the boundaries which limit its own jurisdiction. . . . No one, we believe, has ever doubted the proposition, that, according to the institutions of this country, the sovereignty in every State resides in the people of the State, and that they may alter and change their form of government at their own pleasure. But whether they have changed it or not by abolishing an old government, and establishing a new one in its place, is a question to be settled by the political power. And when that power has decided, the courts are bound to take notice of its decision, and to follow it.[26]

Chief Justice White, in *Pacific States Telephone and Telegraph Company* v. *The State of Oregon*,[27] was faced with the question whether the adoption of the initiative and refer-

---

[25] *Ibid.*, 39.   [26] *Ibid.*, 47.   [27] 223 U. S. 118 (1912).

endum was compatible with the constitutional requirements
of a government republican in form. Like Taney in the pre-
ceding case, White upheld the decision of the lower court
primarily on grounds of expediency.

In the first place, it was the opinion of the court that if
the arguments of the defendant company were sound, "the
validity, not only of the particular statute . . . but of every
other statute passed in Oregon since the adoption of the initiative and referendum," [28] would necessarily be affected.
Secondly, "however perfect and absolute may be the establishment and dominion in fact of a state government, however complete may be its participation in and enjoyment of
all its power and rights as a member of the national government, and however all the departments of that government
may recognize such state government, nevertheless, every
citizen of such state, or person subject to taxation therein,
or owing any duty to the established government, may be
heard, for the purpose of defeating the payment of such taxes
or avoiding the discharge of such duty, to assail in a court
of justice the rightful existence of the state." [29] As a result
of this, said Chief Justice White, "it becomes the duty of
the courts of the United States, where such a claim is made,
to examine as a justiciable issue the contention as to the
illegal existence of a state, and if such contention be thought
well founded, to disregard the existence in fact of the state,
of its recognition by all of the departments of the Federal
government, and practically award a decree absolving from
all obligation to contribute to the support of, or obey the
laws of, such established state government." [30]

This language leads one to believe that Chief Justice White,
even had he ignored, or knew nothing of, the precedent set
by *Luther* v. *Borden,* and anticipating the confused legal
consequences of a decision upholding the proposition that
"by the adoption of the initiative and referendum, the state
violates the right to a republican form of government which
is guaranteed . . . by the Federal Constitution," would have

---

[28] *Ibid.,* 141.   [29] *Ibid.,* 141-142.   [30] *Ibid.,* 142.

considered the opposite more expedient; all the more so, since
the initiative and referendum had been in effect in Oregon
since 1902.   What Justice White did when he placed the
whole question in the category of political questions was to
dismiss the case for lack of jurisdiction and, in so doing,
to maintain the *status quo*.

Texas v. *White* [31] presents what would seem to be an
anomalous situation with regard to the doctrine of political
questions.   It will be remembered that one of the questions
presented to the Supreme Court in this case was whether
or not a state government existed in Texas after the col-
lapse of the Confederacy, and which was privileged to bring
suit before the court.   The court was cognizant of the fact
that in keeping with precedent it could not decide the question.   Yet, paying lip-service to the doctrine of political
questions, the court at the same time decided that the government of Texas was privileged to sue and that because
Congress in passing the Reconstruction Acts had recognized
the provisional government as established.

It may be of advantage in the understanding of this case
to refer to a letter written to John Russell Young [32] by
Chief Justice Chase, who rendered the decision of the court.
In this letter Chase said:

> I start with the premises that Congress has full power to govern
> the rebel States until they accept terms of restoration which will in-
> sure future loyalty, the fulfillment of national obligations, the repudi-
> ation of all rebellion and the obligations of rebellion; and the se-
> curity of all rights for all men; and that the acts of Congress must
> be construed with reference to these ends, liberally; [but] I don't
> want to see Congress set aside the provisional State governments.
> It would be a very mischievous measure in its effects on private
> rights, and lead to much litigation, and very seriously retard, I fear,
> the restoration of order and prosperity to the South.   Congress may
> well provide that the military commander may remove State officials
> who put themselves in the way of reconstruction; and that their suc-
> cessors may be elected by *universal suffrage*, but I would not have
> military commanders authorized to appoint their successors, unless
> temporarily. . . .[33]

---

[31] 7 Wall. 700 (1869).
[32] In Robert B. Warden, *An Account of the Private Life and Public
Services of Salmon Portland Chase*, p. 667.
[33] *Ibid.*, pp. 667-668.

In another communication, this time to August Belmont,[34] Chase said:

> I would eradicate if possible every root of bitterness. I want to see the Union and the Constitution established in the affections of all the people, and I think that the initiative should be taken by the successful side in the late struggle. I have been and am in favor of so much of the policy of Congress as bases the reorganization of the State governments in the South upon universal suffrage.[35]

Suppose the Supreme Court *had* decided that the provisional government representing Texas was not privileged to bring suit in the Supreme Court. The court then would have subscribed, or voiced approval, of either the "State Suicide"[36] theory of Sumner, the "Conquered Province"[37] theory of Thaddeus Stevens, or the "Forfeited Rights"[38] theory. And it may be questioned whether, in Chase's mind, judicial approbation, particularly the approbation of the highest court in the land, of the military courts and military governments, bizarre travesties of representative government, not to mention governmental corruption and maladministration, would have furthered the restoration of "order and prosperity to the South."[39] To be sure, private rights were actually violated and did lead "to much litigation,"[40] and the glowing success of the Radicals in Congress after the election of 1866 undoubtedly did "seriously retard"[41] rehabilitation in the South; but, had the Supreme Court decided the case of *Texas* v. *White* otherwise than it did, it would have played into the hands of the radicals who maintained that because of secession and rebellion, the former Confederate states were no longer states of the Union, but conquered territory and to be treated as such. In other words, the Supreme Court subscribed to the "presidential theory" of restoration, a theory first held by Lincoln and later by Johnson, and according to which, "the Union was legally

---

[34] In Jacob W. Schuckers, *The Life and Public Services of Salmon Portland Chase*, p. 584.

[35] *Ibid.*, p. 586.

[36] Westel W. Willoughby, *The American Constitutional System*, p. 88.

[37] *Ibid.*, p. 89.   [38] *Ibid.*

[39] From letter, Chase to Young. Warden, p. 668.

[40] *Ibid.*   [41] *Ibid.*

indestructible, and that, therefore, the Southern States had never been out of the Union." [42] By this theory, though the previously rebellious states were still to be considered states of the Union, they possessed no constitutional governments, and such being the case, *ipso facto,* they possessed no constitutional rights. Therefore, the first need of these disqualified states was the reestablishment of governments which were loyal and republican in form. And so it was declared, "in the performance of this task the General Government . . . might constitutionally lend its aid, but might not impose a controlling will." [43]

Thus, it is, perhaps, not improper nor unreasonable to assume that Chase and his associates wished to attain certain results, a certain state of things, born out of practical considerations. At least it would seem that the court desired to salvage the old Confederate states from a position of legal inferiority, and as the letters of Chase indicate, accelerate rehabilitation of the political, social, and economic activities of the Southern states. In order to assist in the attainment of these consequences the court had some difficulty with the Reconstruction Acts which specifically declared that no legal governments existed in the ex-Confederate states. But the court held that the authority for the reconstruction activities of the government had been derived from the guaranty clause, so for the purposes of the court it was only necessary to determine whether or not Congress in passing the Reconstruction Acts had recognized the provisional government of Texas as established. In the opinion of the court this had been done, and for the purposes of the court it was sufficient. Texas recovered from White and others the bonds which had been utilized in waging a rebellion against the authority of the United States.

In the first two cases considered above it is evident that the prime factor underlying the use of the doctrine of political questions was expediency; a desire on the part of the court to avoid any possible conflict with the political departments.

---

[42] *Willoughby,* p. 88.   [43] *Ibid.*

In the Texas case, likewise, expediency played a part; but here, the purpose of the court would seem to have been the attainment of certain legal and social consequences affecting the relations between the Union and the former Confederate states, which consequences the Congress did not deem desirable. To do this, the court played loosely with the political question involved, and ignored the precedent set by *Luther* v. *Borden*, but to which Chase paid lip service. Had the court, in the application of the doctrine, abided by the decision of Congress, the social consequences aspired to by the court would have been but a vain hope. As it was, though the court did not admit it, the court actually decided the question thereby making it possible for the state to sue at the bar of the Supreme Court.

In the Indian cases also it would seem that a social factor underlies the use of political questions. The doctrine lent itself beautifully to the realization of desirable social consequences; at least, it is not unreasonable to assume that the results anticipated by the Supreme Court justices were by them deemed desirable.

In *Cherokee Nation* v. *Georgia*,[44] the Supreme Court was asked to issue an injunction against the State of Georgia to prevent the execution of certain laws destructive to the political integrity of the Cherokee Nation. It so happened that before the case was heard in the Supreme Court, an event occurred in Georgia, significant in its consequences. George Tassels, a Cherokee, was convicted in a Georgia court for the murder of another Indian. While awaiting execution, however, a writ of error,[45] bearing the signature of John Marshall, was obtained from the Supreme Court, giving order to the state to show cause why the conviction of Tassels by the state court should stand. This, Georgia bluntly refused to do. And the Georgia legislature resolved as a consequence that "the interference by the chief justice of the supreme court of the United States, in the administration of the criminal laws of this state . . . is a flagrant vio-

---

[44] 5 Pet. 1 (1831).
[45] *Niles' Register*, XXXIX, 338.

lation of her rights," [46] that the governor, and all other officials of the state, are "hereby requested and enjoined, to
disregard any and every mandate and process that has been
or shall be served upon him or them, purporting to proceed
from the chief justice or any associate justice of the supreme
court of the United States, for the purpose of arresting the
execution of any of the criminal laws of this state," [47] that
"his excellency the governor be . . . authorized and required, with all the force and means placed at his command
. . . to resist and repel any and every invasion from whatever quarter, upon the administration of the criminal laws
of this state," [48] and that the governor be empowered "to
communicate to the sheriff of Hall county, by express, so
much of the foregoing resolutions, and such orders as are
necessary to ensure the full execution of the laws, in the
case of George Tassels. . . ." [49]   A few days later, Tassels
was hanged. [50]

A rebellious attitude on the part of the legislature of
Georgia was, undoubtedly, nothing new to Marshall and his
associates.   In 1793, the Supreme Court, in *Chisholm* v.
Georgia, [51] had held that, under the terms of the Constitution, the judicial power of the Federal government should
extend to all cases "between a State and citizens of another
State." [52]   The resentment aroused by this decision is common knowledge; but previous to the adoption of the eleventh
amendment, [53] the Georgia House of Representatives expressed its resentment in no uncertain terms.   In the Journal of the House, November 19, 1793, there appeared the
following:

And be it further enacted that any Federal marshal, attempting to
levy on the territory of this State, or on the treasury, by virtue of an
execution, by the authority of the Supreme Court of the United
States, for the recovery of any claim against the said State of
Georgia shall be guilty of a felony, and shall suffer death, without
benefit of clergy, by being hanged. [54]

---

[46] *Ibid.*   [47] *Ibid.*   [48] *Ibid.*   [49] *Ibid.*
[50] *Ibid.*, p. 353.   [51] 2 Dall. 419 (1793).   [52] Art. 3, sec. 2.
[53] The eleventh amendment became effective February 7, 1795.
[54] Quoted in Ulrich B. Phillips, *Georgia and State Rights*, pp. 27-
28. This enactment of the House, however, was not adopted by the
Senate.

In the instant case, however, the Supreme Court, defied and insulted by the State of Georgia, could do nothing, since Jackson, as the chief executive, would not uphold the authority of the court. Jackson's sympathies lay with the State. " There is no constitutional, conventional, or legal provision," said Jackson in his first annual message, " which allows them [55] less power over the Indians within their borders than is possessed by Maine or New York." [56]   Jackson, it may be said, directly assisted Georgia in its course as regards the Cherokees. This is clearly indicated in a letter written by the governor of the state to the general assembly:

> I transmit to both houses of the general assembly, copies of a communication received from the war department,[57] in answer to a letter requesting of the president the withdrawal of the United States troops from the territory of the state, occupied by the Cherokees. . . . The legislature will perceive in the conduct of the president in this matter, as well as all others, the disposition to accord to Georgia all her rights.[58]

In addition, there was a distinct breach between the administration and the Supreme Court. Jackson opposed the growing power of the court and its appellate jurisdiction: " Congress, the Executive, and the Court must each for itself be guided by its own opinion of the Constitution." [59]   In his message vetoing the renewal of the charter of the United States Bank, and with particular reference to the opinion of Marshall in the case of *McCulloch* v. *Maryland*,[60] Jackson said:

> It is as much the duty of the House of Representatives, of the Senate, and of the President to decide upon the constitutionality of any bill or resolution which may be presented to them for passage or approval as it is of the supreme judges when it may be brought before them for judicial decision. The opinion of the judges has no more authority over Congress than the opinion of Congress has over the judges, and on that point the President is independent of both. The authority of the Supreme Court must not, therefore, be per-

---

[55] Alabama and Georgia.
[56] Richardson, *Messages and Papers of the Presidents*, III, 1020.
[57] The communication referred to was written by Secretary of War Eaton. *Niles' Register*, XXXIX, 263.
[58] *Ibid.*
[59] Richardson, III, 1145.
[60] In which Marshall upheld the constitutionality of the previous charter.

mitted to control the Congress or the Executive when acting in their legislative capacities, but to have only such influence as the force of their reasoning may deserve.[61]

A movement was even afoot in Congress to repeal the 25th section of the Judiciary Act. Jackson and Marshall stood at opposite poles; the former, a believer in State Rights,[62] "the product of a fresh upheaval of democracy," [63] the latter, on the whole federalist with firm belief in "national supremacy," representing the "static forces of society." [64]

Why did the court decide the case of *Cherokee Nation* v. *Georgia* in this way? The dissenting opinion of Mr. Justice Thompson clearly indicates that the court could have granted the injunction. Concluding his opinion, Justice Thompson said:

I am of opinion: (1) That the Cherokees compose a foreign State within the sense and meaning of the Constitution, and constitute a competent party to maintain a suit against the State of Georgia. (2) That the bill presents a case for judicial consideration, arising under the laws of the United States, and treaties made under their authority with the Cherokee Nation, and which laws and treaties have been and are threatened to be still further violated by the laws of the State of Georgia. . . . (3) That an injunction is a fit and proper writ to be issued to prevent the further execution of such laws, and ought therefore to be awarded.[65]

Why did Marshall, who, as a youth had held the Indians in such high esteem that he willingly supported the plan, conceived by Patrick Henry, of white amalgamation with them,[66] leave the Cherokees to the mercy of Georgia? On October 29, 1828, Marshall wrote the following to Story:

The conduct of our forefathers in expelling the original occupants of the soil grew out of so many mixed motives that any censure which philanthropy may bestow upon it ought to be qualified. The Indians were a fierce and dangerous enemy whose love of war made them sometimes the aggressors, whose numbers and habits made them

---

[61] Richardson, III, 1145.
[62] However, not as respects nullification.
[63] Beveridge, *Life of John Marshall*, IV, 466.
[64] *Ibid.*
[65] 5 Pet. 80. Justice Story concurred in this dissent.
[66] "We have rejected some bills, which in my conception would have been advantageous to the country. Among these, I rank the bill for encouraging intermarriages with the Indians." Marshall to Monroe, December 1784, Monroe Papers, MSS. Quoted in Beveridge, I, 241.

formidable, and whose cruel system of warfare seemed to justify every endeavor to remove them to a distance from civilized settlements. It was not until after the adoption of our present government that respect for our own safety permitted us to give full indulgence to those principles of humanity and justice which ought always to govern our conduct towards the aborigines when this course can be pursued without exposing ourselves to the most afflicting calamities. That time, however, is unquestionably arrived, and every oppression now exercised on a helpless people depending on our magnanimity and justice for the preservation of their existence impresses a deep stain on the American character. I often think with indignation on our disreputable conduct (as I think) in the affair of the Creeks of Georgia. . . .[67]

And in the second paragraph of Marshall's opinion, the sympathy for the Indian is apparent: "If courts were permitted to indulge their sympathies, a case better calculated to excite them can scarcely be imagined." [68]   Why, again the question is asked, did Marshall, who so dominated the court,[69] dismiss the case for lack of jurisdiction?

What might have been the possible consequences had Mr. Justice Thompson's opinion been the opinion of the majority?   From the foregoing, it might, without vagary, be said that the grant of an injunction by the Supreme Court, issued to prevent the further execution of the laws of Georgia in the Cherokee territory, would have been ignored both by the State of Georgia and by the President.   A short time previously, Georgia had ignored a writ of error issued by the Supreme Court and defied its authority; and the legislature of Georgia, to add insult to injury, had resolved that " every mandate and process . . . purporting to proceed from the chief justice or any associate justice of the supreme court of the United States, for the purpose of arresting the execution of any of the criminal laws of this state," [70] should be disregarded by the governor and other state officials.   Add to this the attitude of the President toward the court. Whatever the decision, without the assistance of the execu-

---

[67] Charles C. Smith, "Letters of Chief Justice Marshall," *Proceedings of the Massachusetts Historical Society*, 2nd Series, XIV, 337-338.

[68] 5 Pet. 15.

[69] "No man had ever a stronger influence upon the minds of the others." *American Jurist*, XIV, 242. Quoted in Beveridge, IV, 60.

[70] *Niles' Register*, XXXIX, 338.

tive, the laws of Georgia would have prevailed over the
Cherokees. Knowing this, is there reason to believe that
Marshall would willingly have placed the court in a position to receive insult and defiance from a recalcitrant state,
which defection he knew to be inevitable?

But, it would seem, considering this case together with
the case which follows, that a broader purpose lay behind
the decision of Marshall. *Worcester* v. *Georgia* [71] concerned
two missionaries, Samuel A. Worcester and Elizur Butler,
who refused to secure a license to remain in the Cherokee
territory as required by Georgia law. The missionaries were
arrested, convicted, and sentenced to imprisonment at hard
labor. They finally appealed to the Supreme Court of the
United States. In *Cherokee Nation* v. *Georgia* [72] the majority of the court dismissed the action on the ground that
the court lacked jurisdiction over the parties; and as Marshall said in the opinion, " it savors too much of the exercise of political power to be within the proper province of
the judicial department." [73] In the *Worcester* case Marshall
declared the Cherokee acts of the Georgia legislature unconstitutional. " The Cherokee Nation, then, is a distinct community, occupying its own territory, with boundaries accu-
rately described, in which the laws of Georgia can have no
force, and which, the citizens of Georgia have no right to
enter but with the assent of the Cherokees themselves or
in conformity with treaties and with the acts of Congress.
The whole intercourse between the United States and this
nation is, by our Constitution and laws, vested in the government of the United States." [74] Thus the Supreme Court
held that the jurisdiction of the Federal government over
the Cherokees was exclusive and that the State government
had no power over them or their territory. In other words,
to quote Louis L. Jaffe, " in a controversy over the rights
of a private party, and clearly within its jurisdiction, the
court decided the very ' political question ' it had abjured
the previous session. It interpreted certain documents con-

---

[71] 6 Pet. 515 (1832).
[72] 5 Pet. 1 (1831).

[73] *Ibid.*, 20.
[74] 6 Pet. 561.

taining agreements between the United States and the Cherokees; it decided that these documents were 'treaties'; that
by these treaties the United States had guaranteed the political autonomy of the Cherokees; that the acts of Georgia
were violations of the treaties. The executive was not con-
sulted, and legend has it that he might have decided otherwise." [75]

Marshall rejected the State Rights theory upon which
Georgia had acted; he asserted that an Indian tribe " cannot maintain an action in the courts of the United States "; [76]
he interposed the dictum that " if it be true that the Cherokee Nation have rights, this is not the tribunal in which
those rights are to be asserted. If it be true that wrongs
have been inflicted, and that still greater are to be apprehended, this is not the tribunal which can redress the past
nor prevent the future "; [77] finally, Marshall placed the Indian question in the category of political questions and under
the jurisdiction of the Federal government. [78] By all these
means Marshall removed the control of the Indian and his
lands from the states to the Federal government—in his mind,
perhaps, the lesser of two evils.

This policy, as evidenced by the cases, [79] has been consistently maintained by the Supreme Court. " Taking these
decisions together," says Mr. Justice Day, " it may be taken
as the settled doctrine of this court that Congress, in pursuance of the long-established policy of the government, has
a right to determine for itself when the guardianship which
has been maintained over the Indian shall cease. It is for
that body, and not the courts, to determine when the true
interests of the Indian require his release from such condition of tutelage." [80]

---

[75] *Judicial Aspects of Foreign Relations*, p. 19.
[76] *Cherokee Nation* v. *Georgia*, 5 Pet. 20 (1831).
[77] *Ibid.*
[78] *Worcester* v. *Georgia*, 6 Pet. 515 (1832).
[79] See for example, *United States* v. *Holliday*, 3 Wall. 407 (1866);
United States v. *Forty-three Gallons of Whiskey*, 93 U. S. 188 (1876);
United States v. *Sandoval*, 231 U. S. 28 (1913).
[80] *Marchie Tiger* v. *Western Investment Company*, 221 U. S. 286
(1911).

If we turn to foreign affairs we shall find several factors of utmost importance underlying the utilization of the doctrine of political questions. First of all, the conduct of foreign affairs has been considered by the courts as vested in the political departments. To be sure, Mr. Justice Clarke in the case of *Oetjen* v. *Central Leather Company*,[81] involving the question of the recognition of a foreign government, has said that " the conduct of the foreign relations of our government is committed by the Constitution to the executive and legislative—' the political '—departments of the Government, and the propriety of what may be done in the exercise of this political power is not subject to judicial inquiry. . . ." [82] But many questions concerning the foreign relations of the United States, questions of recognition, of the interpretation of treaties, of jurisdiction over territory, might well have come within the purview of the courts had the courts so decided. In such matters, however, it was only reasonable and expedient that the courts should have acted in unison with the political departments. " The national will," said District Judge Dietrick with particular reference to the recognition of Russia, " must be expressed through a single political organization; two conflicting ' governments ' cannot function at the same time. By the same token, discordant voices cannot express the sovereign will of the American nation. Either the executive or the judiciary must be superior in a given sphere." [83] Obviously, if such were not the case, occasions might arise in which the political departments would be at loggerheads with the judiciary, say over a question of territorial jurisdiction. As Justice M'Lean said in the case of *Williams* v. *Suffolk Insurance Company*,[84] " if this were not the rule, cases might often arise in which, on the most important questions of foreign jurisdiction, *there would be an irreconcilable difference between the execu-*

---

[81] 246 U. S. 297 (1918).

[82] *Ibid.*, 302. With regard to this view, see Melville Weston, " Political Questions," *Harvard Law Review*, XXXVIII, 296.

[83] The *Rogdai*, 278 Fed. 294 (1920). See also Quincy Wright, *The Control of American Foreign Relations*, pp. 13-68.

[84] 13 Pet. 415 (1839).

tive and judicial departments. By one of these departments, a foreign island or country might be considered as at peace with the United States, whilst the other would consider it in a state of war. No well regulated government has ever sanctioned a principle so unwise, and so destructive of national character." [85] Chief Justice Taney said with reference to the negotiation of treaties that " it would be impossible for the Executive Department of the government to conduct our foreign relations with any advantage to the country, and fulfill the duties which the Constitution has imposed upon it, if every court in the country was authorized to inquire and decide whether the person who ratified the treaty on behalf of a foreign nation had the power, by its Constitution and laws, to make the engagements into which he entered. . . ." [86] It is true, also, that the courts might be unable to agree among themselves.

In the case of *In re Cooper,*[87] which involved the question of the jurisdictional limits of the United States over the Behring Sea, the Supreme Court, accepting the limit set by the political departments, declared that the jurisdiction of the United States extended to a line far beyond the customary three-mile limit. It may be well to examine briefly certain contemporary developments which were taking form in our relations with Great Britain.

With the declaration of the government of the United States that her jurisdiction extended almost to the middle of the Behring Sea, and the subsequent capture of British vessels upon the open sea, on the ground of violation of an act of Congress, the British government protested vigorously. A settlement of the dispute was attempted through ordinary diplomatic channels, but without success. The United States assumed the position that the Behring Sea " was not included in the term ' Pacific Ocean ' as used in the correspondence on the subject of the Russian ukase of 1821 and that therefore neither the United States nor Great Britain

---

[85] *Ibid.,* 420. Italics my own.
[86] *Doe* v. *Braden,* 16 How. 657 (1853).
[87] 143 U. S. 472 (1892).

had questioned Russia's exclusive jurisdiction over Behring Sea."[88] Great Britain, on the other hand, presented a contrary attitude, and consequently declared that Russia had "acquired no rights by prescription, and that the United States in attempting to close Behring Sea was relying on the discredited doctrine of *mare clausum*."[89] The dispute was finally submitted to arbitration by the convention of February 29, 1892,[90] and over a year later, August 15, 1893, an award was made, unfavorable to the claims of the United States.[91] Now, in the midst of this controversy, it is hardly probable that a court of the United States would have handed down a decision which in effect would have tended to undermine the position of its own government. Had the Supreme Court done so, we should have had the extremely anomalous picture of the judiciary pitted against the executive and legislative departments in a matter affecting international relations. We should have had contradictory attitudes where a unified front was essential. And, last but not least, the case presented by the United States would not have held water, and would have redounded to the advantage of Great Britain, had the highest court of the United States declared the position assumed by its own government to be faulty. This is a practical factor, a factor always to be borne in mind, in such a question as this. In *In re Cooper,* a case *involv*ing so ticklish a question, for the court to relegate the problem of jurisdiction to the realm of political questions and accept the determination of the political departments, seems eminently expedient and practicable.

If the courts could sit in judgment of the political departments and their decisions affecting foreign relations "what an anomaly would such interference present to the world."[92] Here Justice Washington was referring to the public charac-

---

[88] John H. Latané, *A History of American Foreign Policy*, p. 468.
[89] *Ibid.*
[90] Treaties, Conventions, International Acts, Protocols and Agreements between the United States of America and Other Powers, 1776-1909, comp., W. M. Malloy, I, 746.
[91] *Ibid.*, p. 751.
[92] *United States* v. *Ortega*, Fed. Cas. 15,971 (1825).

ter of a foreign minister, but the applicability of the statement touches all the phases of foreign affairs discussed in
this work.

Another factor, candidly expressed by Justice Iredell in
a case involving the violation of a treaty, is extremely significant. It had been contended that should Congress declare a treaty violated by another power, the Congress would,
therefore, be encroaching upon the jurisdiction of the judiciary. "Such a thing," said Justice Iredell, "was never in
the contemplation of the Constitution. If it was, a method
is still wanting by which it could be executed; for, if we
are to declare, whether Great Britain or the United States,
have violated a treaty we ought to have some way of bringing both parties before us." [93]

Justice Iredell's statement, however, is only partially correct. It must not be forgotten that many cases involving
political questions, involve private parties as well. This being the case, the court could execute its judgment upon them.
Assume for the moment that the Supreme Court in *Oetjen* v.
Central Leather Company [94] completely ignored the action of
the political departments and decided that the Carranza government was not the *de jure* government of Mexico. Such
a decision, the reverse of that actually handed down by the
court, could have been enforced because the parties to the
suit were private parties and, along with the property concerned, under the jurisdiction of the courts of the United
States.

The courts will not hesitate to assume jurisdiction over a
controversy where private justiciable rights are involved, in
spite of the presence of questions of extreme political significance. In fact, the Supreme Court has asserted that it
cannot decline such jurisdiction. In the case of *In re
Cooper* [95] the Supreme Court held itself bound by the posi-

---

[93] *Ware* v. *Hylton*, 3 Dall. 199, 261 (1796). See also *Kennett* v.
Chambers, 14 How. 38 (1852), where it was held that a "judicial
tribunal is wholly unfit" to decide a question of recognition. See
also *Taylor* v. *Morton*, Fed. Cas. 13,799 (1855).

[94] 246 U. S. 297 (1918).

[95] 143 U. S. 472 (1892).

tion assumed by the political departments. None the less, Mr. Justice Fuller declared that " we are not to be understood, however, as underrating the weight of the argument that in a case involving private rights, the court may be obliged, if those rights are dependent upon the construction of acts of Congress or of a treaty, and the case turns upon a question, public in its nature, which has not been determined by the political departments in the form of a law specifically settling it, or authorizing the executive to do so, to render judgment, since we have no more right to decline the jurisdiction which is given than to usurp that which is not given." [96]

---

[96] *Ibid.* Cf. *Cherokee Nation* v. *Georgia*, 5 Pet. 1 (1831), and *Worcester* v. *Georgia*, 6 Pet. 515 (1831).

CHAPTER V

CONCLUSION

This study was begun with the purpose of examining various controversies involving political questions which had come before the Supreme Court of the United States. It was the purpose to observe the doctrine of political questions, as it were, in action; to note the consequences when the court enshrouded a question in the folds of this doctrine; and finally, to discover the motives of jurists in so placing a problem within the category of political questions and then accepting the decision of the political departments. In other words, the interest has been directed toward the problem of purposes and consequences rather than toward principles and theories. While invoking the doctrine of political questions, judges have upon occasion, perhaps unconsciously, brought to light the underlying purposes and the consequences aspired to, so artfully hidden by a self-created, elaborate and persistent Newtonian structure of law.[1] It is behind the screen that we find the essence of our subject.

First of all, it must be evident from a review of the cases that when a court declares a question to be a political question, it disclaims all jurisdiction and authority over the question and accepts the decision of the political departments, whether this decision be expressed by act of Congress, official statement or declaration, or treaty, though such decision may well be found in the absence of such expressions. This constitutes the immediate effect of the application of the doctrine of political questions.

It has been declared that courts cannot decide political questions because of a dearth of rules. Without rules, so runs the thesis, the courts are impotent. Again, it has been held that the courts disclaim all jurisdiction over political questions because their final decision lies with the electorate. Finally, the doctrine of the separation of powers has been

---

[1] See Frank, *Law and the Modern Mind*, ch. xii.

invoked by the courts to uphold the contention that certain questions are non-justiciable and, therefore, must be decided by the political departments under whose jurisdiction they fall. None of these explanations, it has been found, is sufficiently satisfactory to constitute the *raison d'être* of political questions, and the accusations respectively of unrealistic, false and doctrinaire must stand against them.

Thus, secondly, it has become evident that underlying the utilization of the doctrine there is something more than theory. The question of the status of Indian tribes was labeled a political question in order to accord the scattered tribes of redmen a unity of attitude on the part of the Federal government. The latter, not the individual states, dealt with the Indians until the second half of the last century, by means of treaties since the tribes were considered quasi-sovereign nations; and it is apparent that to determine the status of a particular tribe the courts should turn to the political departments of the Federal government within whose jurisdiction lay the problem. But also, it seems not unreasonable to assume that Marshall in *Cherokee Nation* v. *Georgia* and *Worcester* v. *Georgia,* in first denominating the status of Indian tribes a political question, was motivated by the claims of social justice. As Professor W. W. Willoughby has said, " it has, however, been held by the Supreme Court that the General Government has an authority over the Indians not springing from specific grants of power, aside from the general treaty-making power, but from the practical necessity of protecting the Indians and the non-existence of a power to do so in the States." [2] To uphold this statement, Professor Willoughby cites the case of *Cherokee Nation* v. *Georgia.* Again, it was certainly a manifest expediency that led the Supreme Court in *Luther* v. *Borden* to sustain the contemporary government of Rhode Island by the use of the doctrine of political questions, and to accept the attitude of the political departments of the Federal government toward that state government. This attitude was expressed, not only

---

[2] *The Principles of the Constitutional Law of the United States,* p. 198.

in the action of the president, but in the fact that the senators and representatives of that state government had been found acceptable to the Senate and the House, both of which, by the terms of the Constitution, determine the qualifications of their own members.

In the Reconstruction case of *Mississippi* v. *Johnson*,[3] the doctrine of the separation of powers was not the only reason for the court's refusal to enjoin the executive. There was another reason why the court threw the problem into the category of political questions; to quote Chief Justice Chase, " suppose the bill filed and the injunction prayed for allowed. If the President refuse obedience, it is needless to observe that the court is without power to enforce its process." [4]

Most questions, labeled " political questions " by the courts, concern, however, matters of foreign relations. It would seem obvious that for practical reasons, for reasons of expediency, some body or organs of government constituting a unity must represent the official attitude of the United States toward foreign nations. Were a treaty to be interpreted by the judiciary as well as by the political departments, a foreign nation would hardly know which interpretation to accept as valid and official. Were the political departments, for example, to declare a certain territory within the jurisdiction of the United States, while the judiciary denied the jurisdiction claimed, foreign governments would be perplexed, to say nothing of the dilemma which would exist within the limits of our own governmental system. It seems, therefore, not unreasonable to conclude that when the courts denominate a question of foreign relations a political question, its purpose is to concentrate the decision of such questions in the hands of what may be deemed, considering the purposes, one governmental organ, in order that as a consequence, the attitude of the United States may be explicit and consistent. This is a very practical matter both in its purposes and its effects.

In its effect, the English act of State is similar to our political question. The act of State is limited to the field

---

[3] 4 Wall. 475.   [4] *Ibid.*, 500-501.

of foreign relations, but in this field, " all that the Crown does . . . falls within the category of acts of State." [5] A decision of the Crown in foreign affairs is accepted without question in any British court. In *Buron* v. *Denman*,[6] the defendant, an officer in the Royal Navy, made a treaty with the chief of an uncivilized country for the abolition of the slave trade. This was done without the authority of the Crown. In pursuance of the terms of the treaty the officer and his men committed what were deemed to be acts of aggression on the plaintiff's property. The court, however, held that the subsequent ratification by the Crown of the unauthorized treaty made what would otherwise have been illegal, an act of State, and that consequently, the plaintiff possessed no right of action against the defendant. In *Salaman* v. *Secretary of State for India*,[7] it was said that " an act of State is essentially an exercise of sovereign power, and hence cannot be challenged, controlled, or interfered with by municipal Courts. Its sanction is not that of law, but that of sovereign power, and, whatever it be, municipal Courts must accept it, as it is, without question." [8] An act of the Crown in foreign affairs may be " just or unjust, politic or impolitic, beneficial or injurious, taken as a whole, to those whose interests are affected. These are considerations into which their Lordships cannot enter. It is sufficient to say that, even if a wrong has been done, it is a wrong for which no Municipal Court of justice can afford a remedy." [9]

Political questions, though similar to some extent with respect to subject matter, must not be confused with the non-justiciable question of international law. Viscount Bryce describes the term " justiciable " as applied to " disputes as

[5] D. L. Keir and F. H. Lawson, *Cases in Constitutional Law*, p. 298.
[6] 2 Exch. Rep. 167 (1848).
[7] 1 K. B. 613 (1906).   [8] *Ibid.*, 639.
[9] *Secretary of State for India* v. *Kamachee Baye Sahaba*, 13 Moore, Privy Council, 22, 86 (1895). See also *Walker* v. *Baird*, A. C. 491 (1892); *Johnstone* v. *Pedlar*, 2 A. C. 262 (1921); *Duff Development Company* v. *Kelantan Government*, A. C. 797 (1924). For a detailed and scholarly treatment of the English act of State see W. Harrison Moore, *Act of State in English Law*.

to the interpretation of a treaty, as to any question of international law, as to the existence of any fact which, if established, would constitute a breach of an international obligation, or as to the nature and extent of the reparation to be made for any such breach." [10] These cases, Bryce contends, admit of arbitration. Nevertheless, since many questions of a non-legal sort arise from the effort of one nation to effect a change in the legal set-up of its foreign relations, it is clearly evident that all disputes cannot yield to arbitration.[11] For instance, the immediate, and to be sure, unimportant, causes of the Franco-Prussian war of 1870, would hardly have admitted of arbitration. The French ambassador, Benedetti, objected arrogantly to the election of a Prussian prince, Leopold, to the vacant throne of Spain, insisting that the "vital interests" of France were at stake. The King of Prussia withdrew the name of his relative, but the French demanded, in spite of this, that Leopold should never become a candidate for the Spanish throne. The King of Prussia rejected this proposal, and then informed Bismarck, in the famous Ems telegram,[12] of Benedetti's demand and his own action in regard to it. Bismarck, given permission to inform the press and the Prussian embassies abroad of the demands of France, and being desirous of precipitating a war with France, cunningly garbled the King's message with the result that France and Germany each thought itself insulted by the other. This dispute was purely political in the sense that there seemed to be no question of disputed fact or law amenable to arbitration. Nor would the underlying causes have been any the more susceptible to an arbitral tribunal. As Brierly has so well said:

At any moment an international incident might arise out of the insistence on the Monroe doctrine by the United States, the dissatisfaction of Germany with her Eastern frontiers, the ambition of Italy for more colonial territory, the desire of Spain for exclusive control

---

[10] *International Relations*, p. 221. See also J. A. Hobson, *Towards International Government*, pp. 34-35.

[11] The term "arbitration" is here used in what Brierly calls "its proper sense"; that is, "the process of settling disputes according to rules of law." See J. L. Brierly, *The Law of Nations*, p. 185.

[12] Robert H. Lord, *The Origins of the War of 1870*, ch. vi.

of Tangiers; but any of these problems would raise an essentially *political* question, susceptible of amicable settlement no doubt, but only by appropriate *political* methods, by negotiations, by compromise, by mediation or conciliation; there is not the smallest chance that they would or could be settled by the *ipso dixit* of an arbitrator.[13]

The essential difference between the political question of constitutional law and that of international law lies in the fact that the former applies to questions arising in the course of deciding cases in our national and state courts, while the latter applies to disputes between foreign nations which may or may not be considered suitable for settlement by an international tribunal. Furthermore, it is not the arbitrator who decides whether the point at issue is a political issue, but the political departments of each party to the dispute.[14]

Finally, a word may be said about the doctrine of political questions and judicial review. Professor Edward S. Corwin in his recent work, *The Twilight of the Supreme Court,* states that the " doctrine of political questions signalizes an early concession by the Court itself at the expense of the strict logic of judicial review. . . ."[15] This statement is true in so far as it relates to a case like *Luther* v. *Borden;*[16] but it would hardly apply to a question concerning the date of the beginning of a war, for example. In this type of case, there being no question of the executive or the Congress acting in excess of constitutional power, there is no question of judicial review. Within limits, therefore, the judiciary has made concessions at the expense of judicial review, but concessions founded in the inadequacy of the judiciary itself. The political questions of today might well have been justiciable questions had the Supreme Court so de-

---

[13] Brierly, p. 186. See also William B. Hornblower, " How Far are Wars Preventable by Judicial Arbitration? " *Proceedings of Third National Conference American Society for Judicial Settlement of International Disputes, 1912,* p. 209.

[14] See Pitman B. Potter, " The ' Political Question ' in International Law in the Courts of the United States," *Southwestern Political and Social Science Quarterly,* VIII, 127. See also addresses on the distinction between legal and political questions by Charles G. Fenwick, Edwin M. Borchard, and Quincy Wright, in *Proceedings of the American Society of International Law,* 1924.

[15] p. 111.   [16] 7 How. 1 (1849).

cided. If the court found it better to limit its jurisdiction, to restrict its power of review, it was not because of the doctrine of the separation of powers or because of a lack of rules, but because of expediency. If the court left certain questions pertaining to foreign relations in the hands of the political departments, it was because in our foreign relations a unified front is sensible, practical and expedient. If the court placed the question of whether a state of the Union possessed or did not possess a republican form of government within the jurisdiction of the political departments, it was because of very practical considerations. If the court was fully conscious that its mandate could not, or would not, be enforced in the particular case, obviously it was more expedient to leave the matter to the political departments exclusively. In general, judicial review or not, the court has found it more expedient to leave the decision of certain questions to governmental bodies more appropriately adapted to decide them.

In fact, many questions, now deemed justiciable by the Supreme Court, may at some future date be considered political questions because of the " felt necessity " [17] to realize anticipated consequences. If as a consequence of a change of economic conditions, certain problems of government, now within the jurisdiction of the judiciary, might more effectively be settled by the political departments, it would seem likely that the Supreme Court would denominate such problems political questions. Certainly, where necessity requires the concentration of decision in the political departments, the court will find a useful category in the doctrine of political questions.

---

[17] Oliver W. Holmes, *The Common Law*, p. 1. See also John Dewey, " Logical Method and Law," *Cornell Law Quarterly*, X, 17.

BIBLIOGRAPHY

PRIMARY SOURCES

Federalist, The (E. H. Scott, editor), 2 vols., Chicago, 1894.
Laws of the United States of America, Washington, 1805, VII.
Martens, George F. de, *Nouveau recueil de traités*, Gottingue, 1818, III.
————, *Nouveau recueil de traités*, Gottingue, 1831, VI.
Moore, John B., *A Digest of International Law*, 8 vols., Washington, 1906.
Poore, Benjamin P., *The Federal and State Constitutions, Colonial Charters, and Other Organic Laws of the United States*, 2 vols., Washington, 1877.
Proceedings of the Hague Peace Conferences, Conference of 1907, 3 vols., New York, 1920.
Richardson, James D., ed., *A Compilation of the Messages and Papers of the Presidents*, 18 vols., Washington, 1900.
Smith, Charles C., " Letters of Chief Justice Marshall," *Proceedings of the Massachusetts Historical Society*, Second Series, XIV, 320-360, November, 1900.
Statutes at Large of the United States.
Story, Joseph, *The Public and General Statutes Passed by the Congress of the United States of America from 1789 to 1836 Inclusive*, 4 vols., 2d ed. (George Sharswood, editor), Philadelphia, 1837.
Treaties and Conventions Concluded between the United States of America and Other Powers (John H. Haswell, compiler), Washington, 1889.
Treaties, Conventions, International Acts, Protocols and Agreements between the United States of America and Other Powers, 1776-1909. 2 vols. (W. M. Malloy, compiler), Washington, 1910.
U. S. Congress, *Congressional Record*, 38th Congress, 1st session, 65th Congress, special session, 74th Congress, 2d session.
————, *House Documents*, no. 121, 20th Congress, 2d session; no. 91, 23d Congress, 2d session.
————, *House Report*, no. 262, 43d Congress, 1st session.
————, *Senate Document*, no. 62, 55th Congress, 3d session.
U. S. Department of State, *Foreign Relations of the United States*, 1910.
U. S. Supreme Court, *Reports.*

SECONDARY SOURCES

Barry, Frederick, *The Scientific Habit of Thought*, New York, 1927.
Beveridge, Albert J., *The Life of John Marshall*, 4 vols., Boston, 1929.
Bondy, William, *The Separation of Governmental Powers*, in " Columbia University Studies in History, Economics and Public Law," New York, 1896, V, no. 2.
Borchard, Edwin M., *The Diplomatic Protection of Citizens Abroad, or the Law of International Claims*, New York, 1915.
————, " The Distinction between Legal and Political Questions," *Proceedings of the American Society of International Law, 1924*, pp. 50-56.

131

Borchard, Edwin M., " The Unrecognized Government in American Courts," *American Journal of International Law*, XXVI, 261-271, April, 1932.

Bowers, Claude, *The Tragic Era*, Boston, 1929.

Brierly, J. L., *The Law of Nations. An Introduction to the International Law of Peace*, Oxford, 1928.

Bryce, James (Viscount), *International Relations*, New York, 1922.

Canfield, G. F., " The Legal Position of the Indian," *American Law Review*, XV, 21-37, January, 1881.

Cardozo, Benjamin N., *The Nature of the Judicial Process*, New Haven, 1928.

———, *The Growth of the Law*. New Haven, 1927.

Connick, Louis, " The Effect of Soviet Decrees in American Courts," *Yale Law Journal*, XXXIV, 499-510, March, 1925.

Cook, Walter Wheeler, " Scientific Method and the Law," *Johns Hopkins Alumni Magazine*, XV, 213-236, March, 1927.

———, " ' Substance ' and ' Procedure ' in the Conflict of Laws," *Yale Law Journal*, XLII, 333-358, January, 1933.

Cooley, Thomas M., *The General Principles of the Constitutional Law of the United States*, 4th ed. (Andrew A. Bruce, editor), Boston, 1931.

Corwin, Edward S., *The Twilight of the Supreme Court; a History of Our Constitutional Theory*, New Haven, 1934.

Cox, Isaac J., *The West Florida Controversy, 1798-1813. A Study in American Diplomacy*, Baltimore, 1918.

Dewey, John, *Human Nature and Conduct. An Introduction to Social Psychology* (Modern Library Edition), New York, 1930.

———, " Logical Method and Law," *Cornell Law Quarterly*, X, 17-27, December, 1924.

———, *The Quest for Certainty*, New York, 1929.

Dicey, Albert V., *Lectures on the Relation between Law and Public Opinion in England during the Nineteenth Century*, London, 1926.

Dickinson, John, " Legal Rules: Their Function in the Process of Decision," *University of Pennsylvania Law Review*, LXXIX, 833-868, May, 1931.

Dunn, Frederick S., *The Protection of Nationals*, Baltimore, 1932.

Dunning, William A., *Reconstruction, Political and Economic*, New York, 1907.

Eagleton, Clyde, *International Government*, New York, 1932.

Eddington, Arthur S., *The Nature of the Physical World*, New York, 1930.

Fairlie, John A., " The Separation of Powers," *Michigan Law Review*, XXI, 393-436, February, 1923.

Fenwick, Charles G., " The Distinction between Legal and Political Questions," *Proceedings of the American Society of International Law*, 1924, pp. 44-50.

———, *International Law*, New York, 1924.

Field, Oliver P., " The Doctrine of Political Questions in the Federal Courts," *Minnesota Law Review*, VIII, 485-513, May, 1924.

Foster, John W., *The Practice of Diplomacy*, Boston, 1906.

Frank, Jerome, *Law and the Modern Mind*, New York, 1930.

" Georgia and the Cherokees," *Niles' Register*, XXXIX, 338-339, 1830-1831.

" Georgia and the Indians," *Niles' Register*, XXXIX, 263-264, 1830-1831.

Gray, John C., *Nature and Sources of the Law*, New York, 1916.

Haines, Charles G., " General Observations of the Effects of Personal, Political, and Economic Influences in the Decisions of Judges," *Illinois Law Review*, XVII, 96-116, 1922-1923.

Henderson, John B., *American Diplomatic Questions*, New York, 1901.

Hobson, John A., *Towards International Government*, London, 1915.

Holmes, Oliver W., *Collected Legal Papers*, New York, 1921.

———, *The Common Law*, Boston, 1881.

———, " The Path of the Law," *Harvard Law Review*, X, 457-478, March, 1897.

Hornblower, William B., " How far are Wars Preventable by Judicial Arbitration?" in *Proceedings of the Third National Conference American Society for Judicial Settlement of International Disputes, 1912*, pp. 209-228, Baltimore, 1913.

Jaffe, Louis L., *Judicial Aspects of Foreign Relations, In Particular of the Recognition of Foreign Powers*, Cambridge, 1933.

Keir, D. L. and Lawson, F. H., *Cases in Constitutional Law*, Oxford, 1928.

Latané, John H., *A History of American Foreign Policy*, New York, 1929.

Lehman, Irving, " The Influence of the Universities on Judicial Decision," *Cornell Law Quarterly*, X, 1-16, December, 1924.

Lord, Robert H., *The Origins of the War of 1870, New Documents from the German Archives*, Cambridge, 1924.

Mathews, John M., *The Conduct of American Foreign Relations*, New York, 1922.

Meriam, Lewis and Associates, *The Problem of Indian Administration*, " Institute for Government Research Studies in Administration," Baltimore, 1928.

Moore, W. Harrison, *Act of State in English Law*, New York, 1906.

Mowry, Arthur M., *The Dorr War; or, the Constitutional Struggle in Rhode Island*, Providence, 1901.

———, " One Treaty Ratified," *New York Times*, March 14, 1925.

Oppenheim, L., *International Law*, 2 vols., 4th ed. (Arnold D. McNair, editor), London, 1926.

———, " Pass Pines Treaty Giving Isle to Cuba," *New York Times*, March 14, 1925.

Phillips, Ulrich B., " Georgia and State Rights," *Annual Report of the American Historical Association, 1901*, II, 15-224.

Phillipson, Coleman, *Termination of War and Treaties of Peace*, New York, 1916.

Pierson, William W., " Texas *versus* White," *Southwestern Historical Quarterly*, XVIII, 341-367, April, 1915, XIX, 1-36, July, 1915.

Potter, Pitman B., " The ' Political Question ' in International Law in the Courts of the United States," *Southwestern Political and Social Science Quarterly*, VIII, 127-142, September, 1927.

Randall, James G., *Constitutional Problems under Lincoln*, New York, 1926.

Ritchie, A. D., *Scientific Method, an Inquiry into the Character and Validity of Natural Laws*, New York, 1923.

Schiller, Ferdinand C. S., *Logic for Use*, New York, 1930.

Schroeder, Theodore, " The Psychologic Study of Judicial Opinions," *California Law Review*, VI, 89-113, January, 1918.

Schuckers, Jacob W., *The Life and Public Services of Salmon Portland Chase*, New York, 1874.

Snow, Alpheus H., *The Question of the Aborigines*, New York, 1921.

Snow, Freeman, *Treaties and Topics in American Diplomacy*, Boston, 1894.

Taft, William H., *Our Chief Magistrate and His Powers*, New York, 1925.

Warden, Robert B., *An Account of the Private Life and Public Services of Salmon Portland Chase*, Cincinnati, 1874.

Warren, Charles, *The Supreme Court in United States History*, 3 vols., Boston, 1922.

Weston, Melville, " Political Questions," *Harvard Law Review*, XXXVIII, 296-333, January, 1925.

Wharton, Francis, *A Digest of the International Law of the United States*, 3 vols., Washington, 1887.

Willoughby, Westel W., *The American Constitutional System*, New York, 1917.

———, *The Constitutional Law of the United States*, 3 vols., 2nd ed., New York, 1929.

———, *Principles of the Constitutional Law of the United States*, 2nd ed., New York, 1930.

Wright, Quincy, *The Control of American Foreign Relations*, New York, 1922.

———, " The Distinction between Legal and Political Questions with Especial Reference to the Monroe Doctrine," *Proceedings of the American Society of International Law, 1924*, pp. 57-67.

TABLE OF CASES

INDEX

Act of State, English, 126 ff.
Adger v. *Alston*, and the termination of war, 45.
Alagon, Duke of, and *Doe* v. *Braden*, 65, 66.
Alaska, 91 ff.
Alexandria County, Virginia, 96.
Alien Property Custodian, 49.

Baiz, Ex parte, cited, 63.
Behring Sea, 91 ff., 120-121.
Benson v. *United States*, and the boundaries of a military reservation, 96-97.
Bentall v. *United States*, cited, 48.
Beveridge, Albert J., cited, 68, 115, 116.
Bismarck, 128.
Bondy, William, cited, 13.
Borchard, Edwin M., cited, 44, 61, 129.
Botiller v. *Dominguez*, and the violation of treaties, 74-75.
Brewer, Mr. Justice, and *Wilson* v. *Shaw*, 88-90; and *Benson* v. *United States*, 96-97.
Brierly, J. L., and the political question in international law, 128-129.
Bryce, Viscount, and the nonjusticiable question in international law, 127-128.
Buena Ventura, the, cited, 37.
Buron v. *Denman*, and the English act of State, 127.

Camfield v. *United States*, cited, 30.
Campbell, Mr. Justice, 94.
Campbell v. *New York Evening Post*, and judicial rules, 101.
Canfield, G. F., cited, 28; on the Indian and the treaty-making power of the President, 30-31.
Cardozo, Mr. Justice Benjamin N., on *Hynes* v. *New York Central Railroad Company*, 100-101; on *Oppenheim* v. *Kridel*, 101; on the judicio-legislative relation, 103.

Carranza government, 58, 59, 60, 122.
Chambers, General T. J., vide *Kennett* v. *Chambers*.
Charlton v. *Kelly*, and the termination of treaties, 78-79.
Chase, Chief Justice, and *Texas* v. *White*, 23-27, 109-112; and the *Protector*, 39; letter of, to John Russell Young, 109; letter of, to August Belmont, 110; and *Mississippi* v. *Johnson*, 126.
Cherokee Nation v. *Georgia*, background of, 31-32; decision, 32-33; relation of, to case of George Tassels, 112-113; and the attitude of Andrew Jackson, 32, 114; dissenting opinion of Mr. Justice Thompson, 115, 116; and *Worcester* v. *Georgia*, 117-118; cited, 123.
Cherokee Tobacco, the, and the violation of treaties, 71-72; cited, 75.
Christophe, government of, and *Gelston* v. *Hoyt*, 52-54.
Civil War, American, commencement of, 38-44; termination of, 45-47.
Clarke, Mr. Justice, 119.
Clinton v. *Englebrecht*, cited, 30.
Coke, Lord, 101.
Columbia, Republic of, 89.
Congress, and the guarantee of a republican form of government, 18; and *Texas* v. *White*, 24-25, 109 ff.; and the readmission of Texas, 26; and the legal status of Indian tribes, 27 ff.; the joint resolution of, July 2, 1921, 49; and treaties, 69 ff.
Conley v. *Ballinger*, cited, 30.
Connick, Louis, cited, 61.
Consul of Spain v. *The Conception*, cited, 54.
Cook, Walter Wheeler, 102, 105.
Cooley, Thomas M., on republican form of government, 16.